Speedy Gourmet

by C. Norman Shealy, M.D., Ph.D.

Illustrated by Mark Peyton

BRINDABELLA BOOKS
Columbus, Ohio — Fair Grove, Missouri

TABLE OF CONTENTS

Introduction 7

Real Foods, Real Quality 9

Planning Ahead 33

Breakfasts 57

Lunches 109

Dinners 151

Desserts 205

Special thanks to Hal Huggins, D.D.S.,
who suggested the title,
and to my son Craig,
who proofed and helped add comments

Speedy Gourmet

Dedicated to Real Food—
a rarity in American cuisine

INTRODUCTION

Cooking—and eating—should be fun. If they are not, then the cooking is not likely to be done well and the eating is, at best, humdrum. I enjoy both, but I choose to cook mostly simple meals—meals which taste good, are nutritious, and are quick to prepare. Years of experience have convinced me that fast food can be good food, too—and good for you. I have acquired the "speedy gourmet" habit—and so can you.

The freedom of being at home, the clean air of home, the better quality of home-cooked food, and the *time saved* are all reasons why I strongly prefer home cooking. By the time you travel any distance to a restaurant (even a "fast food" one), wait to be served, wait to get your check, and travel home, it is unlikely that your meal out has taken less than an hour. The Speedy Gourmet solves this problem by cooking at home. All of the meals in this book are designed to be prepared in a minimum of time. The fact that they are less expensive and more nutritious than restaurant meals is an extra bonus.

The recipes included in this book give enough suggestions to prepare different meals for breakfast, lunch, and dinner for three months. That's a lot more variety than you'll find in restaurants! But before we put the soup on, there are some basic principles of being a Speedy Gourmet that need to be addressed:

The *quality* of the food we fix and eat.

Planning ahead to use your time wisely. The time you would otherwise spend traveling and waiting for a meal out can be used to plan and create a nutritious meal at home.

Stocking up on food and equipment.

Exploring alternatives—the art of substituting.

I hope you will use this book not as a standard cookbook, but as a kitchen companion, as though I were standing in your kitchen chatting with you as you cooked. That is the way I have written it.

So let's go into the kitchen—the kitchen of the Speedy Gourmet!

—C. Norman Shealy, M.D., Ph.D

REAL FOODS,
REAL QUALITY

The greatest revolution in nutrition in the history of the world has led, in just the last forty years, to a precipitous decline in the quality of the food we eat. The home cooked meal has been replaced by packaged foods, convenience foods, soft drinks, processed foods, frozen foods, and fast foods, changing the face of American nutrition. Salt intake, for example, has increased in the last twenty-five years to a whopping ten grams per person each day, about four times what is optimally healthy. The annual consumption of refined sugar has increased from approximately one pound per person one hundred and thirty years ago to one hundred and twenty-eight pounds per person today.

Why has this revolution occurred? Because we like being able to "eat and run," and we are willing to sacrifice quality and nutrition in exchange for speed and convenience. Five percent of the total food dollar is spent at vending machines; one-third is spent at fast food restaurants. Even at home, we consume far more sugary, processed cereals, candy, and highly salted convenience foods than we do "real food." *Over one billion dollars is spent each year to promote processed foods, while virtually nothing is spent advertising real food.*

I am not a purist; I recognize the fact that it is difficult to eat *only* real food in a busy lifestyle. But we should understand the value of proper nutrition, and strive for the ideal as much as possible.

Actually, the greatest problem of the modern American diet may not be the high level of intake of salt, sugar and fat, but its extreme limitation of variety. By the mid-1970's, fat provided 42 percent of all calories consumed by the average American; sugar represented 18 percent. Both of these are whopping increases since early in the century. The incidence of degenerative diseases and cancer is strongly related to the unbalanced consumption of these unreal and incomplete foods, which are highly prevalent in the fast food industry.

Sadly, consumption of the most important food of all, complex carbohydrate or starch, dropped 45 percent during the same time. In part, this is because these foods tend to seem rather bland to the average Westerner, who has become accustomed to a great deal of fat, refined sugar and refined starch. Unless one is prepared to become a food faddist, sacrificing both taste and convenience, it is not possible to achieve what would nutritionally be considered an "ideal diet." Since this alternative is unappealing to most of us, the emphasis in this cookbook will be on combining good taste and convenience with excellent nutrition.

Chart I helps tell the story of nutrition. It shows the consumption of food by category in the American diet at present, in the ideal diet, and in the practical and attainable diet of the Speedy Gourmet. The average American diet is the product of eating fast foods and convenience foods; the diet of the Speedy Gourmet, by contrast, emphasizes quick, good-tasting meals of *real food*. The 3 percent sugar and white flour will be that which you cannot avoid in dining out occasionally.

CHART I

	Average American Diet	Ideal Diet	Speedy Gourmet Diet
Fat	42%	10%	25%
Refined sugar	18%	0%	3%
Refined starch (white flour)	18%	0%	3%
Protein	12%	10%	12%
Real Starch (fruit, vegies)	10%	80%	57%

Even with the overall decline in nutrition, Americans today live fifty percent longer than eighty years ago. This is because the human body is amazingly tolerant. Interestingly, *most* of this increase in longevity has resulted from the progress that has been made in improving conditions during the first two decades of life. These gains have lulled us, perhaps, into taking the importance of nutrition for granted. Yet the evidence is overwhelming that poor nutrition (an excess of fat and sugar, plus an inadequate amount of fiber) is one of the strongest factors in degenerative diseases—coronary artery disease, diabetes, varicose veins, hemorrhoids, osteoarthritis, gallstones, high blood pressure, diverticulosis, and cancer of the colon. And cancer of the breast is related to the extremely high level of fat intake in the average American diet.

These startling facts about nutrition have made me a strong advocate of *real food*. I define real food as any food that has not been chemically altered by processing. Unreal food—food that has been chemically altered in one way or another, and thereby robbed of much of its nutritive quality—is any food which bears one or more of the following labels on its packaging:

artificial	sugar or sucrose
processed	corn sweetener
flavored	white flour
partial(ly)	preserved
hydrogenated	retard
hardened	substitute
enriched	refined

All soda pop, for instance, is total junk. Not only is there no real food in it, but it is loaded with phosphate of soda in addition to the usual sugar and caffeine. As a result, the consumption of pop adversely affects calcium metabolism. There are some fairly good substitutes for pop—Jogger Juice™, available from Self-Health Systems of Brindabella Farms (see appendix), and Potent-C™ by Nature's Plus, available at health food stores. These are not perfectly real, but they have a much sounder basis than any pop.

Since we've started with drinks, I should cover coffee, tea and cocoa. They do have caffeine, so you should drink a *maximum* of two cups per day and none after 3 p.m. Rombout's uses a water process to make a wonderful coffee which is 99 percent decaffeinated; it is available at health food stores.

Water quality in this country is a disaster. In *any* city, I would recommend either a stainless steel or glass distiller, or one of the excellent filters such as Water Dome.™ A Culligan™osmotic exchange purifier is a third possibility. But *do not* use artificially softened water; it is loaded with salt and sometimes with cadmium. Even if you have a well you should have the water checked for chemical contamination. Good water should be your *priority* drink. Whole fruit juices and herb teas are next best in quality.

Juices made from fresh fruits, or those frozen or canned without sugar, are best. For instance, a pint of sliced peaches, blenderized with a tablespoon of honey and one pint of water, makes a magnificent drink. All fruits lend themselves to this kind of "quickie" preparation, and the cost is below that of frozen orange juice concentrate—which is definitely inferior in quality to fresh orange juice. Another favorite of mine is rhubarb juice. One pint of cooked rhubarb, blenderized with three tablespoons of honey and three pints of water, makes a great treat.

When it comes to solid food, Charts II and III delineate the kinds of food to consider. Chart II lists foods that should be the cornerstone of your diet; Chart III lists "food concentrates."

CHART II
The cornerstone of a good diet

Grains	Vegies	Legumes
Wheat	Asparagus	Peanuts
Corn	Lettuce	Soybeans
Rice	Kale	Alfalfa seeds
Rye	Chard	Mung beans
Oats	Spinach	Garbanzoes
Barley	Celery	Navy beans
Millet	Tomatoes	Kidney beans
Buckwheat	Cucumbers	Pinto beans
Triticale	Green beans	Red beans
	Cauliflower	Green peas
	Celeriac	Lentils
Starchy Vegies	Eggplant	Aduki beans
	Shallots	Black beans
Irish potatoes	Horseradish	Blackeyed peas
Sweet potatoes	Leeks	Guar beans
Winter squash	Kohlrabi	
Parsnips	Artichokes	
Turnips	Onions	
Carrots	Garlic	
Beets	Broccoli	
Rutabagas	Cabbage	
Arrowroot	Mushrooms	
Okra	Brussels sprouts	
Parsley	Edible podded peas	
Peppers	Sugar snap peas	
Salsify	Jerusalem artichokes	
	Summer squash	

16

Some of the foods listed in Charts II and III may be unfamiliar to you, but they are all commercially available in this country. *At least 75 percent of the foods you eat should come from the four categories in Chart II, which is why I call it the "cornerstone of a good diet."* Actually, it is possible to have a perfectly nutritious diet by eating only foods from Chart II, but it would be necessary to take vitamin B_{12} supplements. Adding eggs, dairy products, or meat, however, eliminates the problem and most likely produces a more balanced diet. A lacto-ovo vegetarian diet, which includes dairy products and eggs as well as grains, starchy vegies, vegie vegies, and legumes, is certainly a healthy diet—but not any healthier than a diet which includes some quantities of meat.

The food concentrates are over-consumed in this country. Ideally, if you have a well-balanced diet of legumes and grain, you need a minimum of one serving per day of the food concentrates to obtain adequate protein. *Most people should not exceed four servings per day of the food concentrates*, however, because they are extremely high in fat and protein. A serving of any of the meats would consist of two to four ounces; a dairy serving would consist of one glass of milk, four ounces of cottage cheese or yogurt, or one and a half ounces of cheese; and a serving of eggs would be one or two. The variations are determined by one's physical size. Nuts and seeds are very high in fat and protein. I would not recommend more than one or two tablespoons per day.

Fruits are, in a sense, food concentrates of simple

sugar. If you do not eat a lot of refined foods, such as white sugar and white flour, it is probably safe to eat any reasonable amount of fruit. For most people, however, we would suggest about three servings per day.

The energy foods are the grains, starchy vegetables and legumes. The vegie vegies largely provide bulk, vitamins, minerals and a lot of good taste. Meats should also be used to provide taste, flavor and variety, rather than the bulk of a meal. An entree should really be built around the grains, starchy vegetables and legumes, rather than the meats.

Grains can be eaten whole, flaked, rolled, cracked or ground into flour. All of them can be used to make delicious breads, although I recommend using at least thirty percent wheat flour in any bread or pancake recipe, as it gives it a better quality. Nevertheless, pure corn bread can be quite delicious, and rice bread can be made with no wheat at all. The grains are deficient in some of the essential amino acids, so they need to be complemented with legumes, meats, dairy products or eggs. In general, one part legume to four or five parts grain gives a good protein mixture.

Grains and legumes need to be either cooked or sprouted to be properly digested. Most of the starchy vegetables—especially potatoes, sweet potatoes and the winter squashes—are also digested better if they are cooked. All vegie vegetables can be eaten raw, and in fact retain optimal vitamin content when they are eaten raw, but they are also quite delicious steamed and fixed in many other ways.

It would be nice to lay the egg controversy to rest once and for all, but we can only report the facts as they exist in the scientific literature. Except for people who are allergic to eggs, there is no evidence that eggs are at all harmful to anyone except possibly that small percentage of individuals who have "familial hypercholesterolemia." To restrict eggs to the rest of the population is one of the most ridiculous concepts ever proposed, since eggs represent the single most complete food available in the world. One or two eggs per day are perfectly safe and healthy for any individual who does not have familial hypercholesterolemia. It is best, however, that eggs not be eaten fried. As far as the quality of protein is concerned, soft-boiled eggs are probably best of all.

The best quality fats are butter and cold pressed safflower oils. Cold pressed corn oil is also a very good quality oil. I do not recommend using any other commercially available fat for cooking or any other use, except a small bit of lard for preparing pie crust. Actually, pork lard is far better than butter or margarine, and certainly far better than Crisco ®. Crisco and all other solid white vegetable shortenings are inferior forms of fat, as much of the unsaturated fat has been converted into translinoleic acid, which is almost a transvestite. The essential ingredient in oils, cislinoleic acid, is far better for you.

There is no evidence that butter is harmful, and

in fact, basic laboratory research indicates that animals fed margarine develop twice as much atherosclerosis as animals fed butter. All margarines have some degree of artificially saturated or hydrogenated fats which convert the cislinoleic acid to translinoleic acid, so we do not recommend margarines under any circumstance. Also, any peanut butter with artificially hydrogenated fat should be avoided.

The best place to buy a wide variety of legumes and grains is a food co-op. (The Speedy Gourmet will have more to say about co-ops in the next chapter.) Most of the starchy vegetables, vegie vegetables and other foods can be found at regular grocery stores. If you live in the city, you might try to find a friendly farmer nearby who raises meats organically and buy all your meat products (and fresh vegetables) there. And eggs that come from a farm where the hens run around the barnyard taste better than other eggs. Some people feel they have better nutritional value as well, but the research on that issue is incomplete. I recommend that you stock up on legumes and grains. You can buy a three-to-six-month supply and keep it on hand without risk of spoilage.

I do not recommend white sugar for any purpose whatsoever. If you feel you absolutely must have the granulated white sweetening, use fructose, which is even sweeter than regular white sugar. One-half teaspoon of fructose will substitute for one full teaspoon of sugar. I prefer honey, because it reminds you not to use too much! Use two-thirds of a teaspoon of honey for each teaspoon of refined white sugar.

Chart IV, on the next page, lists the average American consumption of a variety of foods per year—with the *daily* average of alcohol consumption as well. The changes I would like to see in the average American diet would be:

• An increase in the consumption of dry beans and peas to at least thirteen pounds per person each year.

• A decrease in candy consumption to a *maximum* of one pound (or none) a year.

• A decrease in total refined sugar intake to a maximum of twenty pounds per year.

• A decrease in coffee drinking to a maximum of 360 cups a year.

• A decrease in the use of margarine to zero.

• A decrease in the consumption of so-called vegetable shortening to not more than six pounds per person each year.

• An increase in fish consumption to at least fifteen pounds each year.

• An increase in total cereal grains to at least 200 pounds per person.

• A decrease in the consumption of ice cream and ice milk to a maximum of two and a half pounds per person.

• A decrease in total red meat to a maximum of fifty pounds per person.

• A decrease in soft drink consumption to zero.

If this book can help achieve these goals, then it will have made a worthwhile contribution.

CHART IV
Average Annual American Consumption

Absolute alcohol	3 gallons
Whiskey	0.9 ounces/day
Wine	0.8 ounces/day
Beer	9.8 ounces/day
Dry beans	6.5 pounds
Dry peas	0.1 pounds
Peanuts	6 pounds
Candy	17 pounds
Sugar (including candy)	128 pounds
Coffee	560 cups
Tea	160 cups
Cocoa	4 pounds
Eggs	276
Butter	4.4 pounds
Margarine	12.5 pounds
Lard	2.6 pounds
Shortening	18 pounds
Fresh & frozen fish and shellfish	8.1 pounds
Canned fish	4.2 pounds
Total cereal grains	140 pounds
Fresh fruit	80 pounds
Frozen fruit	140 pounds
Ice cream and ice milk	28 pounds
Total red meat	165 pounds
Melons	19 pounds
Milk	32 gallons
Cheese	21 pounds
Fresh potatoes	45 pounds

Total "Irish" potatoes . . . . 120 pounds
Total poultry . . . . 52.9 pounds
Soft drinks . . . . 493 8-oz. servings
Total vegetables . . . . 220 pounds
   Processed vegetables . . . . . . 122 pounds
   Fresh vegetables . . . . 98 pounds
Total foods . . . . 1,460 pounds

Most pickles, ketchup (28 percent sugar and loaded with salt), potato chips (60 percent fat and loaded with salt), salted nuts and various "snack" foods are largely artificial, fat, salty and sugared. The fact that these "foods" are staple items at most fast food restaurants demonstrates the problem of eating out. I ate at *the* fast food restaurant once in 1962, and one taste was enough for me to shun it. I recommend you do the same for most fast food restaurants. Actually, most restaurants today, even regular ones, use very artificial "foods" such as Durkee's ® tomato sauce (49 percent sugar, 51 percent chemicals, 0 percent food).

Some of the fast food restaurants now boast a salad bar. Check them carefully and ask pertinent questions. I've been told many restaurants use a chemical spray to keep the salad bar *looking* fresh.

The food at fast food restaurants is not only highly processed and very artificial (especially their milk shakes), but also *emphasizes* the five worst dietary problems: salt, fat, sugar, white flour, and chemical additives. Chart V illustrates some of the worst excesses of fast food.

CHART V
Nutritional Content of Popular Fast Foods

Item	Calories	Protein (grams)	Carbo-hydrates (grams)	Fat (grams)	Sodium (milli-grams)
HAMBURGERS					
Burger King Whopper	606	29	51	32	909
McDonald's Big Mac	541	26	39	31	962
Burger Chef hamburger	258	11	24	13	393
FISH					
Arthur Treacher's fish sandwich	440	16	39	24	836
Burger King Whaler	486	18	84	46	735
McDonald's Filet-O-Fish	402	15	34	23	709
Long John Silver's fish (2)	318	19	19	19	NA
CHICKEN					
Kentucky Fried original dinner	830	52	56	46	2285
Kentucky Fried crispy dinner	950	52	63	54	1915
OTHER ENTREES					
Pizza Hut Thin 'n Crispy cheese pizza (half of 10-inch pie)	450	25	54	15	NA
Pizza Hut Thick 'n Chewy pepperoni pizza (half of 10-inch pie)	560	31	68	18	NA
McDonald's Egg McMuffin	352	18	26	20	914
Taco Bell taco	186	15	14	8	79
Dairy Queen brazier dog	273	11	23	15	868
SIDE DISHES					
Burger King french fries	214	3	28	10	5
Arthur Treacher's cole slaw	123	1	11	8	266
Dairy Queen onion rings	300	8	33	17	NA
Burger King vanilla shake	332	11	50	11	159
McDonald's chocolate shake	384	11	60	9	329
McDonald's apple pie	300	2	31	19	414

NA—Not Available. Source: Copyright 1979 by The New York Times Company. Reprinted by permission. Data supplied by companies.

There are many factors involved in creating a balanced diet. While it is easy to conclude that "fast food" does not provide a healthy diet, it is more difficult to determine just what a healthy diet is. There are some who believe that eighty percent of the food we eat should be alkaline—so that when the food metabolizes, it produces an alkaline residue—with 20 percent acid. This is hard to do and has *not* been proven beneficial. However, it is helpful to know which foods are acid, alkaline or neutral. Chart VI shows the content of various types of food when dried to an ash.

CHART VI

FRUITS	VEGIES	STARCH	PROTEIN	OTHER
Alkaline	*Alkaline*	*Acid*	*Acid*	*Neutral*
Apples	Almonds	Bran	Bacon	Butter
Apricots*	Artichokes	Bread, white	Baking pow-	Buttermilk
Bananas	Asparagus	Bread, rye	der biscuits	Corn oil
Berries	Beans, Lima*	Bread, whole	Barley	Cottonseed
Citron	Beets	wheat	Beef	oil
Cranberries†	Beet tops	Corn, dried	Cheese	Cream
Currants	Brussels	Constarch	Chicken	Custard
Grapefruit	sprouts	Crackers	Clams	Honey
Grapes	Cabbage	Flour, white	Crab	Ice cream
Lemons	Carrots	Pastries	Duck	Lard
Melons*	Cauliflower	Spaghetti	Eggs	Milk, whole*
Oranges	Celery		Fish	Olive oil
Pears	Cucumbers		Lamb	Onions
Persimmons	Endive		Liver	Sugar
Pineapple	Lettuce		Lobster	Syrup
Plums†	Limes		Oysters	
Prunes†	Mushrooms		Pork	
Tangerines	Olives, ripe		Scallops	
	Onions		Shrimp	
	Parsley		Veal	
	Parsnips			
	Peas			
	Peppers		* Reduces acidity of urine	
	Potatoes*		† Increases acidity of urine	

Similarly, there is no scientific evidence to support a vegetarian diet, but a lacto-ovo-vegetarian diet *is* healthy. Of considerably more interest is a good balance of *calcium* to *phosphorus*. Americans eat too much phosphorus, which leads to calcium imbalances. All soda pop, for instance, is phosphate of soda. Most high protein foods are loaded with phosphorus at the expense of calcium. The following chart shows the content of calories, protein, fat, carbohydrates, calcium and phosphorus for one ounce of a variety of foods.

CHART VII

Cal.	Food (one ounce)	Protein	Fat	Carb.	Calcium	Phosph.
52	Salmon	7.7 gm	2.1 gm	0 gm	0 mg	117 mg
46	Beef, lean rump	6.7 gm	2.0 gm	0 gm	3 mg	55 mg
54	Turkey	7.7 gm	2.0 gm	0 gm	2 mg	80 mg
46	Tuna (H_2O pack)	8.0 gm	0.2 gm	0 gm	4 mg	55 mg
20	Tofu	2.2 gm	1.2 gm	0.6 gm	46 mg	468 mg
166	Peanuts	7.4 gm	14.1 gm	5.3 gm	21 mg	114 mg
41	Brown rice	0.6 gm	0.5 gm	7.0 gm	4 mg	8 mg
7	Green beans	0.4 gm	0.04 gm	1.0 gm	10 mg	6 mg
10	Milk, whole	0.5 gm	0.5 gm	0.7 gm	36 mg	24 mg
105	Swiss cheese	7.8 gm	7.9 gm	0.5 gm	262 mg	160 mg
29	Egg	4.7 gm	4.3 gm	4.1 gm	17 mg	58 mg
8	Carrots	0.01 gm	Trace	0.1 gm	7 mg	6 mg
100	Chick peas, dry	6.0 gm	1.4 gm	15.0 gm	43 mg	94 mg
2	Summer squash	0.01 gm	0.01 gm	0.5 gm	7 mg	7 mg
20	Baked potato	0.6 gm	0.02 gm	4.5 gm	2 mg	14 mg
5	Pumpkin	0.15 gm	0.05 gm	1.2 gm	38 mg	4 mg
170	Almonds	5.3 gm	16.4 gm	5.5 gm	66 mg	143 mg
10	Rutabagas	0.3 gm	0.03 gm	2.4 gm	17 mg	8 mg
47	Soybeans	4.1 gm	1.6 gm	4.1 gm	21 mg	51 mg
15	Kale, raw	1.7 gm	0.2 gm	2.5 gm	70 mg	27 mg
15	Yogurt	1.0 gm	0.5 gm	1.6 gm	37 mg	26 mg
10	Amaranth	1.0 gm	0.15 gm	2.0 gm	80 mg	19 mg
9	Snapbeans	0.5 gm	0.06 gm	2.0 gm	1.6 mg	1.2 mg

27

I will complete our discussion of "real food" by borrowing some ideas from Dr. Ross Hume-Hall and his wife, Anne Jones Hall, who have prepared a chart depicting "quality levels of eating." They have subdivided all foods into four quality levels, ranging from level one, which is nutritionally superior, to level four, which is nutritionally inferior. I have adapted their chart (*Copyright © En-Trophy Institute, reprinted by permission*) somewhat for our uses.

LEVEL ONE (*nutritionally superior*):
Fruits: raw and fresh.
Vegetables: raw and fresh.
Grain: raw and sprouted.
Meat: raw, grass-fed beef and free-range chickens. Note: the Speedy Gourmet does not recommend eating meat raw! Raw meat *is* nutritionally superior, but meat needs to be cooked!
Fish: raw.
Eggs: farm fresh, raw (egg nog, etc.)
Dairy: raw yogurt and milk, whole.
Oils, fats: raw, oil-bearing nuts and seeds, eaten whole.
Legumes & seeds: raw and sprouted.
Nuts: raw.
Drinks: spring water, raw vegetable juice, freshly expressed.
Sweeteners: none.

LEVEL TWO (*nutritionally good*):
Fruits: lightly cooked, dried.
Vegetables: lightly cooked—steamed, stir fried,

home-made soups and stews.

Grain: 100 percent whole ground flours, home-baked breads, muffins, crepes, whole brown rice, whole grain porridge lightly done.

Meat: cooked grass-fed beef and free-range chickens.

Fish: fresh, cooked.

Eggs: cooked as lightly as possible, farm fresh.

Dairy: commercial, pasteurized milk, good quality cottage cheese, natural cheese, yogurt made with bacteria still alive.

Oils, fats: sweet raw milk, unsalted butter, unrefined oils mechanically expressed without heat.

Legumes & seeds: baked or cooked until just tender.

Nuts: freshly made whole butters.

Drinks: some herb teas, freshly expressed fruit juices.

Sweeteners: honey, molasses, maple syrup in small amounts, dried fruits (raisins, dates, etc.).

LEVEL THREE (*nutritionally fair*):

Fruits: cooked, canned or frozen in their own syrup.

Vegetables: frozen, cooked.

Grain: whole wheat pasta, white flour, cottony-white commercial bread, white rice.

Meat: good quality hamburger, sausages, ham, grain and drug-forced commercial beef.

Fish: frozen, cooked, canned (tuna, etc.).

Eggs: frozen, powdered (and cooked).

Dairy: Chocolate milk, creamed cottage cheese,

commercial cheese (colored, high in salt), yogurt with dead cultures.

Oils, fats: commercial butter (salted), lard (without BHT).

Legumes & seeds: plain canned, overcooked—cooked then baked in casseroles, refried, etc.

Nuts: dry roasted (no additives), good quality commercial peanut butter.

Drinks: unsweetened frozen concentrated fruit juices, canned vegetable and fruit juices.

Sweeteners: large amounts of honey, molasses, and maple syrup.

LEVEL FOUR (*nutritionally inferior*):

Fruits: pie fillings, jams.

Vegetables: canned, commercial stews and soups, french fries, potato chips.

Grain: commercially prepared cereals, minute rice, frozen pizza and bread dough, boxed white pasta.

Meat: deep-fat fried, luncheon meats (salami, bologna, etc.), frankfurters, canned meat.

Fish: deep-fat fried.

Eggs: egg substitutes (Egg Beaters ®, etc.).

Dairy: evaporated milk, processed American cheese, frozen yogurt, Kraft dinner.

Oils, fats: commercial cooking oils (Crisco, Wesson), margarine.

Legumes & seeds: canned with sugar, oil, and/or additives.

Nuts: roasted in oil, heavily salted, commercial peanut butter containing hydrogenated oils.

Drinks: coffee, tea, soft drinks, fruit drinks (Hi-C, Tang, etc.).

Sweeteners: white sugar, brown sugar.

To master the art of Speedy Gourmet, however, we must do more than just master the rules of good nutrition. We must be able to translate them into good tasting recipes that are easy to fix. When all is said and done, the speed with which meals can be prepared is often a more important consideration than the nutritional value of the food. We have become so accustomed to the concept of fast food that we often view traditional cooking as burdensome and time consuming—even if we recognize it to be healthier. I have presented a brief overview of good nutrition, so that you have some basis for understanding the kind of recipes and meals I present. But my major emphasis throughout the book will be on preparing delicious, wholesome meals *which can be completed in a maximum of thirty minutes.* Many of them will take less than ten.

If you compare the time it takes to go somewhere to pick up fast food—or eat it in a restaurant—thirty minutes is a good investment in better taste and better health. And with most of the recipes in this book, the cost will be only 25 to 30 percent of what you would pay in a fast food restaurant.

It will take some patience and practice to learn how to select and prepare these foods, but the return will be well worth it. Within a year, the program outlined in this book can save hundreds of dollars in food costs *for each family member*, improve your health, and save you time.

What makes the meals presented in this book gourmet? *You* will determine that. I love to experiment—throw in a dash of this, a pinch of that, mix and try. If nothing else, I hope this book will inspire you to experiment, too. I'll give you clues, but no real gourmet cook is happy without trying something new and different.

Happy eating!

PLANNING AHEAD

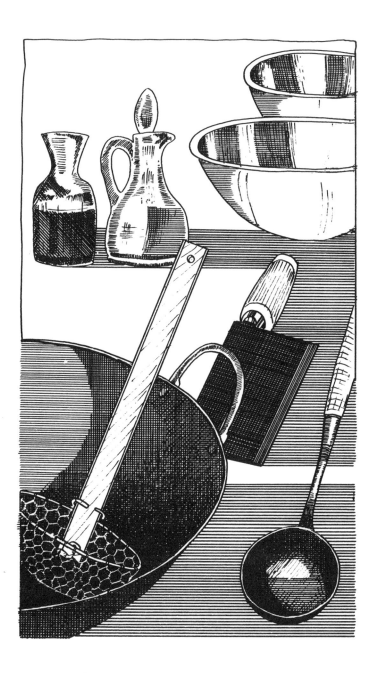

EQUIPMENT

It doesn't take an elaborate kitchen to be a Speedy Gourmet. Most cooks will already have the routine kitchen utensils they will need. But there are a few special ones important enough to mention. Absolute essentials to me are a wire whisk; a blender (Oster or Waring); a slow cooker; a vegetable blanching pot; cast iron frying pans and muffin pans; a stainless steel pressure cooker (about five or six quarts); assorted stainless steel pots; and a food processor. Those who want to prepare their own vacuum packed dried foods can reap a remarkable savings over the cost of buying the same foods already packed, so a home vacuum packer is a nice adjunct—but only if you want to store a year's supply of food at home!

I do not have a microwave oven and probably never will. I am not opposed to it for what it does to food, but I *am* concerned about its radiation effects. And when you look at it from the point of view of cost and how much time it saves, it really doesn't add up to anything worthwhile. So there are no recipes in this book which use a microwave oven—and yet we will still produce speedy, nutritious meals! A convection oven is a nice adjunct, but not essential.

A wire whisk is super for making gravies and sauces, beating eggs, and so on. Some blenders can be used for grinding grains as well as rapid mixing and chopping. Slow cookers allow you the luxury of starting a meal for the evening in the morning, or for anytime the next day the evening before. But whenever a slow cooker is specified, you can achieve the same results by using the settings for "simmer" or "low" on a stove. If your stove cooks too rapidly at those settings, you can purchase inexpensive burner covers to slow or diffuse the heat. Food processors are *great* for chopping salads, mashing potatoes or rutabagas, grating cheese, and so on.

PREPARATION

There are a number of basic principles of food preparation that must be learned by the Speedy Gourmet. One of the most basic is that there are certain foods which must be either cooked or sprouted in order to be digested well by humans. These foods include:

All Grains	*Starchy Vegies*	*Legumes*
Rice	Winter squash	Chick peas
Corn	(pumpkin,	Soybeans
Wheat	acorn, etc.)	Alfalfa seeds
Oats	Irish potatoes	Peanuts
Barley	Sweet potatoes	Navy beans
Rye		Kidney beans
Millet		Pinto beans
Triticale		Lima beans
		Green peas

All *other vegetables* can be easily digested uncooked. The other vegetables, in fact, are *more* nutritious raw—although some *taste* better lightly cooked. There are several ways to prepare food quickly: pan sauteeing, boiling, grilling, broiling, and steaming. Two other techniques that require little preparation time, but must be started hours in advance, are low temperature baking and slow cooking. Other techniques which shorten cooking time are:

1. Increasing the surface area by chopping, grating, grinding or blenderizing the food to be cooked. Blenders and food processors expedite this process.

2. Using a pressure cooker.

Grains, legumes and starchy vegies can be boiled, baked or ground into flour and grilled or sauteed.

Dried beans require several hours or more for baking or boiling; even in a pressure cooker, they require up to two hours. When they are *ground* into a flour, they can be cooked in minutes rather than hours.

Whole grains can be cooked in 20 to 30 minutes. When flaked, rolled, cracked or ground, grains can be cooked in five to ten minutes. This principle of reducing the *size* of food particles or increasing surface area will be used extensively in this book.

Grains can usually be mixed or substituted for one another. It takes very little time or effort to prepare grains whole. If you aren't familiar with millet, it is delicious, nutritious, and a high protein food. You've probably seen it in canary food—

birds often eat better than people! Triticale is a cross between rye and wheat, with improved protein content. Both millet and triticale are likely to be found only at co-ops and health food stores.

Brown rice tastes better than white rice, has more protein and fiber, and cooks as easily as white rice. Here is a pressure cooker recipe for "quick rice" that can be used for any whole grain.

Quick Rice

Place 1 cup brown rice and 2 cups water in a metal or porcelain bowl on a cooking rack in the pressure cooker. Add 1 cup of water to the pot.

Cover and cook at 15 pounds pressure for 5 minutes. Let pressure drop. Remove pressure gauge and simmer 5 more minutes.

Total cooking time for any whole grain will be no more than ten to twelve minutes, using this recipe.

For cooking rice or other grains without a pressure cooker, I offer the following recipe:

Basic Rice

Place 1 cup brown rice (or mixed grains) in a stainless steel pot with 2 cups of water.

Bring pot to a boil and cook rice until the water has been absorbed and bubbles appear on the surface of the rice. Turn heat to lowest simmer and cover. Cook another 5 to 10 minutes before serving.

An innovation of mine is to steam vegetables on

38

top of the rice or grain when it reaches the simmer stage. Almost all vegie vegetables can be prepared in this way, thereby saving a pot and preserving all the nutrients. Even our kids approve!

Here are some other basic recipes which will be referred to throughout the book.

Basic gravy

Heat 1 tablespoon oil in a cast iron pan. Whisk in 2 tablespoons arrowroot flour, add 1 cup milk and cook slowly until thickened.

Yogurt "White Sauce"

1 tablespoon oil
2 tablespoons flour
1 pint (or more) plain yogurt

Mix oil and flour while skillet heats. Stir oil and flour mixture in warm skillet until bubbling well and browned. Stir in yogurt and add seasonings—pepper, salt, soy sauce, or curry—as desired.

Quick Biscuits

Write to Weisenberger Flour Mills, Midway, Kentucky 40347 for information about their wide variety of delicious and excellent quality mixes. A favorite of mine is their "Whole Wheat Biscuit Mix," which I use for these biscuits.

Combine ¼ cup milk with 1 cup mix. Mix until doughy. Turn onto floured board, knead 5 times. Roll to about ⅓ inch (½ inch maximum) thick. Cut with floured cutter or small glass and bake on a greased pan in a 450° oven for 10 to 12 minutes.

If you don't have the "Whole Wheat Biscuit Mix," you

can substitute for it in the following manner:

Use 1 cup blenderized whole wheat flour (blenderizing makes it finer). Add:

1½ teaspoons baking powder
¼ teaspoon salt (or none)
2 tablespoons oil
⅓ cup milk

When well mixed, proceed as above. If you don't want to roll and cut the biscuits, just spoon the mixture onto a greased pan.

Medium Quick Bread

2 envelopes yeast
1 tablespoon honey
2½ cups warm water
7 cups whole wheat flour
1 teaspoon salt

Heat oven to 200°, then turn oven off.

Combine yeast and honey in ½ cup warm water; keep warm on top of stove. Mix flour and salt. Place flour-salt mixture in oven, leaving oven door open. After 10 minutes, remove dough from oven, add yeast mixture, and knead in the remaining water. Knead for 10 minutes.

Shape into loaves and place in two greased 9½ by 5 inch loaf pans. Heat oven once again to 200°, then turn oven off, leaving door half open. Place loaves in oven, let rise. Remove bread from oven. Heat oven to 375°. Return bread to oven, bake for 45 to 50 minutes.

For variety, substitute up to 2½ cups of any ground grain for that amount of wheat flour.

Chapattis

2 cups whole grain flour
1 teaspoon salt
2 tablespoons toasted sesame seeds
Combine with enough water to make a stiff dough. Cook on a hot buttered griddle like pancakes.

Dr. Shealy's Whole Grain Bread

Like Mother used to make!
Mix 1¼ cups warm milk with:
1 package dry yeast
2 tablespoons honey
Let stand for five minutes. Then add:
¼ cup lard or butter or 3/16 cup liquid corn or safflower oil
1 egg
½ teaspoon Lite-salt
Mix well in blender. Then add and mix well 1 cup whole wheat flour, finely ground and blenderized.

Mix in 2½ to 3 cups additional finely ground flour. At least one cup of this amount should be wheat flour; the rest could be rye, triticale, barley, millet, rice, or even corn, if desired.

Knead. Brush top with oil or butter. Let rise. Knead and make into a loaf. Brush top with oil or butter. Let rise. Bake at 350° for 40-45 minutes.

Remove from oven and brush at once with oil or butter. Allow to cool before serving.

The dough can be frozen after the first rise, or baked and then frozen, if that is desired.

Flat Bread (*recipe of* Mabel Hanson, Holmen, Wisconsin)
  2 cups flour
  ½ cup corn meal
  ½ cup graham flour (not necessary, but it makes it much better)
  ¾ pound melted butter
  ½ tablespoon fructose
  1 level teaspoon salt
Mix all ingredients. Pour small amounts of boiling water (be sure to keep it boiling all the time) into the mixture—enough so you can handle it without it sticking to your fingers, but not so much it becomes soupy. Take a tablespoon at a time and roll, roll, roll on a lightly floured surface. Mabel uses a lefse maker, but the bread can also be baked until lightly brown and dry in an oven.

Quickest Bread
  3 cups whole wheat flour
  1 cup corn flour
  1 tablespoon natural baking powder
  ½ teaspoon salt
  2 teaspoons cinnamon
  ¼ cup chopped nuts
  ¼ cup chopped raisins
  1 egg
  1 cup water
Preheat oven to 350 degrees. Combine ingredients slowly, then knead well. Shape into loaves. Brush tops with melted butter. Place on greased baking sheets or in greased loaf pans and bake for 1 hour.

SEASONINGS

The seasoning of food is the personal touch the gourmet cook adds to bring out the full richness of flavor. It is a shame that the average American is addicted to salt, and not just because too much salt is unhealthy—which it is—but also because there are so many other wonderful tastes to explore, once you begin to experiment. I have provided *clues* to good seasoning in the recipes in this book, but hope you will experiment freely. You'll be surprised by what you discover!

In dealing with seasonings, keep in mind that a little goes a long way. Also bear in mind that *mixtures* of a number of seasonings can produce memorable results. Start by seasoning a dish with just one or two condiments, then experiment with additional choices.

Here are some of my favorite seasonings:

Sour cream	Red pepper	Bay leaves	Nutmeg
Yogurt	NoSalt™	Cinnamon	Ginger
Honey	Curry	Cloves	Marjoram
Burgundy	Rosemary	Raisins	Fennel
Sauterne	Thyme	Almonds	Cardamon
Chablis	Dill	Parmesan	Anise
	Basil	Jalapeños	Tarragon
	Sage	All types of	Onion
	Oregano	cheese	Garlic
	Horseradish	Carraway	Spearmint
	Cumin	Allspice	Peppermint
	Lemon	Orange juice	
	extract	concentrate	

A few notes on seasonings:

Red pepper is a very pleasant substitute for black pepper. A little red pepper and salt will enhance all but sweet dishes.

I like to add a touch of honey whenever I use cinnamon or cloves.

Curry needs some salt to bring out the flavor.

When you begin experimenting, go lightly at first, using only a pinch (an eighth teaspoon or less) until you have defined your gourmet tastes.

SUBSTITUTES—
"The art of bluffing"

Every cook needs to know how to substitute one item for another in a recipe. There are times when you are halfway through preparing a meal and you find you are missing an ingredient. Some ingredients just aren't available in every season. And allergies may also require substitutions. Here is a list of substitutes and how to use them:

For Milk (*for cooking purposes*):

1. Dried, skimmed milk, reconstituted.

2. Legume milk—mix any ground legume in water (2 tablespoons per cup) and bring to a near boil while whisking. Can be drunk as well as used in cooking.

3. Nut milk—make as with legume milk. Can be drunk as well as used in cooking.

4. Grain-sesame milk—mix 1 tablespoon each of

ground rolled oats and ground sesame seeds with a cup of water, heat to near boil while whisking. Can be drunk as well as used in cooking.

4. Dried egg white milk—whisk 2 tablespoons dried egg white in 1 cup of water.

5. Grain-gelatin milk—mix 1 tablespoon grain and 1 tablespoon gelatin per cup of water.

6. Yogurt milk—whisk ½ cup yogurt with ½ cup water. For drinking, if you don't like the "buttermilk" flavor, add one teaspoon honey.

For Cream:
Try yogurt. Its texture is slightly different, but with thorough whisking it can be used easily in sauces, soups, casseroles and gravies. But *don't* substitute it for whipped cream. Evaporated milk can be used in place of whipped cream, but it must be *very* cold.

For Meat:
Mix cooked legumes with some grain, milk or eggs to make a "complete" protein.

For Eggs:
Mix 1 tablespoon dried egg white with 2 tablespoons water and 1 teaspoon oil.

For Cooking Oils:
I do not recommend margarine, soy oil, cottonseed oil, linseed oil or any *hydrogenated, solid white* vegetable oil such as Crisco ®, since they are *not* natural foods and/or not as healthy as other oils.

I recommend *only* safflower oil, preferably "cold pressed." Cold pressed corn oil is second best.

Butter can also be used as a substitute for cooking oils, and lard in moderation for pastries. I do not use lard in the recipes in this book, since most pastries require too much time to be considered "speedy." But lard is actually a good substitute for butter when cooking pastries.

Olive oil is not as good in unsaturation and is not recommended, but if you have a strong preference for it, it is okay in small amounts.

For Beef Stock or Bouillon:

1. Blenderize: 1 ounce ground beef, 1 package of gelatin, 1 cup of water, and 1 tablespoon of soy sauce. *In a pinch, you can get by without the ground beef.*

2. Mix 1 tablespoon guar gum, 1 tablespoon soy sauce, and 1 cup of water.

3. Mix 2 tablespoons of ground soy beans or soy flour with 1 cup of water.

For Grain:

In all recipes that do not call for yeast, any grain can be substituted for wheat or any other grain. In yeast recipes, at least 50 percent of the flour should be wheat.

For Baking Powder

Commercial baking powder contains *aluminum*. Americans consume much too much aluminum—in salt, aluminum cans, aluminum pots and pans, aluminum foil and numerous "antacids." Aluminum has been implicated in senility and pre-senile dementia, and I would like to avoid these problems! I recommend *homemade* baking power.

Mix: 1 part baking soda with 2 parts cream of tartar and 2 parts arrowroot flour. Make enough so you can have a batch always on hand.

Arrowroot flour can be found at health food stores or co-ops. It is better than cornstarch for thickening gravies.

I also recommend using cast iron, stainless steel, pottery, porcelain or glass cookware.

For Yeast:

Guar gum provides some rising in flour recipes.

For Salt:

Americans consume *much too much* salt—an average of 10 grams a day, when it should be not more than 2 grams a day. For this reason, salt will not be mentioned in *most* of the recipes in this book. Once you get over the American addiction to salt, you will not want to use very much. Some is required. The flavor of curry is rather bland without some salt. But soy sauce, on the other hand, is *very* salty. You should not add salt any time soy sauce is used. In persons with normal kidneys, it is not necessary or desirable to add salt, even in hot weather. The incidence of high blood pressure is directly related to salt intake, so minimize salt in your diet. Lite salt, K or Co-salt, seasoned salts or kelp can be used at the table in *minimal* amounts as salt substitutes.

STOCKING THE LARDER

It is almost as hard to find real food in most grocery stores as it is in fast food restaurants. Eighty to ninety percent of the stuff sold in the average American grocery is chemicalized, very artificial and non-nutritious. Dr. William Hettler of the University of Wisconsin at Stevens Point has emphasized that you should shop only in the outside lanes of grocery stores, where you'll find meats, dairy products (half processed), fruits, and vegetables. The center lanes contain mostly the real junk, but they do have canned beans and a few useful foods.

Ideally, meats, eggs, vegetables, grains, fruits and milk should be raised on your own or purchased from a reliable "organic" or eco-sound farmer. I strongly recommend that you seek such sources. Form a food co-op, if necessary, or pay someone to obtain *real* food for you. Buy as much as possible from whoever will sell you food that was raised organically, *without poisonous chemicals.*

Health food stores are, in general, a poor substitute. They are useful for grains, some legumes, and sometimes for bread; but they generally lack variety and push a lot of processed junk. *Learn to read, judge and choose!*

At regular grocery stores, buy what you *cannot* purchase from a co-op or a *real food* farmer:

Meats
Butter
Milk

Eggs

Fresh or frozen vegetables, fruits and juices

Breads (although you will rarely find *real* bread in a regular grocery store)

Canned legumes (kidney beans, etc.)

Soaps and kitchen cleaning supplies

Encouragingly, in the last two years I have noticed many grocers have begun stocking more *real* foods. Search carefully. But you'll usually find really good pasta only at a co-op or health food store. Whole wheat spaghetti, especially fidellini, or soy-wheat spaghetti with its terrific protein content, taste good and are much better for you than the inferior white types. And whole grain pasta is cooked exactly the same as the usual stuff.

Let me tell you a little more about food co-ops. "Membership cooperatives" can usually be found in cities of 30,000 or more in population, but the good news is that you often *do not* have to be a member or employee to buy your food there. Many co-ops offer the same food to nonmembers for about 15 percent more than membership prices—but that is still less than you would pay in grocery stores, and the quality of food is usually the best available anywhere but on the farm. *Co-ops are not bastions of flower children!* Information on how to find a co-op is listed in the appendix.

Most co-ops will supply you less expensively with:

Grains of all kinds, including rolled, cracked, flaked, and flours

Legumes (beans and peas)

Old fashioned peanut butter
Pasta (whole wheat or soy-wheat macaroni, spa-
    ghetti, lasagna, etc.)
Breads
Baking powder ingredients
Herbs and spices
Honey
Oils
Soy sauce
Dried fruits
Eggs
Dried milk
Herb teas
Some fresh fruits and vegetables
Yogurt
Cheese
Tofu (try it—you may like it)
Alfalfa seeds and sometimes sprouts
Granola (*rarely* really good or as good as home
    made)
Nuts and seeds

Actually, most co-ops can supply everything except meats, fruits and vegetables (a complete variety in fresh and frozen), and canned legumes (although some may be available).

If you locate a real food farm source for meats, fruits and vegetables, you can buy all your other food at a co-op. I urge you to look for co-ops and a real food farm source. In many cities, the farmers' market fulfills much of the role a co-op plays, as well as supplying eggs, milk, meat, fruit, and vegetables. *But if you aren't interested in co-ops or* natural farmers, don't despair. Most of the recipes in this book can be prepared from items available in grocery stores.

I mention few processed meats—such as ham, bacon and sausage—because the commercial ones are loaded with salt, nitrates and fat. Try to find a source for *real* sausage that is nitrate-free and *all* meat. If you can't, get the *vegetarian* substitutes at a co-op or health food store.

Personally, I consider a well-stocked larder an absolute essential for serious gourmet cooking. I always keep a one-to-three-month supply of the following staples on hand, and would recommend that you do the same:

WHOLE GRAINS

Brown rice	Popcorn
Whole rye	Whole wheat
Barley	Triticale
Millet	Buckwheat groats

FLOURS

Corn meal	Whole wheat
Buckwheat	

CEREALS

Rolled oats	Rolled wheat
Cream of rice	Corn grits
Rice bran	Wheat bran
Wheat germ (*refrigerate*)	Scandinavian flat bread
Noodles	Spaghetti
Lasagna	Macaroni

(*The pasta can be whole wheat, soy wheat, or spinach*)

LEGUMES

Soy beans	Kidney beans
Azuki beans	Lima beans
Pinto beans	Chick peas
Navy beans	Mung beans
Split green peas	Alfalfa seeds (*for sprouts*)
Peanuts	Natural peanut butter

NUTS

Almonds	Walnuts
Pecans	Brazil nuts
Cashews	

HERBS AND SPICES

Pepper	Ginger
Salt	Curry powder
Tumeric	Dried onion and garlic
Nutmeg	Dill weed and seeds
Cinnamon	Thyme
Cloves	Oregano
Rosemary	Sage

HERB TEAS

Spearmint	Lemon grass
Peppermint	Camomile
Red Zinger	Many, many others

OTHER ITEMS

Guar gum—a wonderful thickener that works in hot or cold liquids. A little goes a long way.

Granola—if home made or freshly made. Most commercial granolas are not very exciting.

Tofu—a high protein soy product of moderately-firm custard consistency. It is very bland but can be enhanced by seasonings.

Safflower oil.

Whole grain breads, bagels and English muffins.

PLANNING AHEAD

Even though the recipes included in this book can be *prepared* in less than thirty minutes, many of them do take longer than thirty minutes for the food to *cook*. Mastering the art of Speedy Gourmet therefore involves taking a little time each week to plan ahead and use your time wisely. It may only take five minutes in the morning, for example, to put a main dish into a slow cooker—or a complete meal (roast, vegetables, and potatoes) into a 200° to 250° oven—if you plan ahead. Come suppertime, it only takes another five minutes to set the table and dish up a wonderful meal.

Plan a week at a time. It will take you ten or fifteen minutes, but will save you that much time and more during the week. It will also let you take advantage of vegetable, fruit and meat specials.

And if you plan it well, you can double a recipe and have the next day's lunch from the previous evening's dinner. In Australia, a ''weekend joint'' is a common practice. A large roast or turkey is prepared on Friday with enough vegies to provide lunch and dinner for three days. By Monday, everyone is happy to eat anything else!

53

I have presented enough recipes in this book to have a different breakfast, lunch, and dinner every day for three months. I am a firm believer in food variety. It makes each meal an adventure in gourmet eating—and cooking. By planning ahead, you can extend these meal plans from three months to a whole year—and a new lifestyle of eating! Part of the secret is choosing freely from the vegies to create a wide variety in green salads and steamed vegetables, and complementing your meals with fresh seasonal fruits whenever possible.

The following suggestions for variety can be used as a guide to planning ahead:

Breakfast

An ideal breakfast includes protein, carbohydrate, a fruit or vegetable and good conversation. The following foods can be fixed individually or in combination for an energizing breakfast:

Breads: muffins, rolls, coffeecakes

Cereals: whole, cracked or ground grains

Granola

Eggs: omelets, scrambled, boiled, poached, or baked

Cheese (including cream cheese and cottage cheese)

Fish, fresh or smoked

Pancakes or waffles

Mush

Rice: *boiled* (served hot or cold with cream, milk, yogurt, fruit, raisins, or nuts), *fried* (with eggs, soy sauce, or nuts), or *baked* (as rice pudding).

Millet (boiled like rice and served like cereal)

Rye—whole, ground ("cream of rice" style) or rolled (like oatmeal)

Wheat—*baked* (pancakes, waffles, bread), *rolled* (like oatmeal), or *creamed* ("cream of wheat")

Oats—rolled or steel cut (oatmeal) or boiled, whole

Buckwheat pancakes or bread

Buckwheat groats (boiled as a cereal)

Corn—mush, cornbread or boiled grits

Peanut butter

Scrapple

French toast

Welsh rarebit

Meats

Now, that's variety, compared with the usual American breakfast! Further variety can be gained by combining various grains for cereal or using any combination of grains in breads. Soy flour improves the consistency as well as the protein quality of whole wheat.

Lunch and Dinner

The key to variety in lunches and dinners lies in using the wide range of grains and vegetables available to us with small quantities of meat.

All of the cereal grains, for example, can be used in soups, casseroles, loaves, and salads, opening up great possibilities for variety.

Remarkable variety can also be achieved by using tomatoes and other vegetables as the focal point of main dishes (instead of meat) and flavoring dishes with yogurt, herbs, and other seasonings.

Desserts

The final touch of the meal is also a good way to introduce variety into gourmet eating. Here are some of the possibilities:

Fresh fruits—whole, sliced, baked, pureed
Dried fruits
Pies and tarts
Yogurt with fruits, nuts, seeds
Cakes
Cookies
Sweet breads made with honey
Cobblers
Custards
Puddings
Mousses
Crepes
Frozen yogurt with honey
Homemade ice cream

Confections—peanut butter coconut balls, apricot nut balls, date delights and date treats, halvah.

BREAKFASTS

The healthy Speedy Gourmet never wants to overlook breakfast. Breakfast is an important meal, because it breaks what is essentially a twelve-hour fast. I am not a believer in fasting for most people, and I see no reason to prolong the overnight fast any longer by skipping the morning meal. It needs to be broken, and it should be broken with a tasty, nutritious meal that will stick with you until lunch. Adequate protein and complex carbohydrate are essential for this important meal. As with most meals, whole grains provide an outstanding basis for a *real* breakfast.

As important as this meal is, most people eat rather dull breakfasts, without much variety or choice. I've included some unusual menus to help you begin thinking of breakfast as a *real* meal. Frankly, I enjoy starting the day by experiencing different tastes. But if Spanish rice, curried rye and pork chops sound too mid or late day, try them for brunch or at a different meal. They are still nutritious, tasty, and fast to fix, no matter when you eat them!

I prefer some kind of fruit or fruit juice at breakfast, but would add that it is just as good between meals or with any meal. As with all suggestions, *try it*—you may be pleasantly surprised.

Many of these meals can be started in a few minutes and then left to cook while you shower and dress for the day. Most do not require *watching*.

Choose the ones that sound the most appealing to experiment with first.

All meal recipes are for two servings.

1. Oatmeal

Stir ⅔ cup rolled oats into 2 cups cold water. Bring to a boil in a double boiler. Stir occasionally. Cover and let sit two to five minutes.

Serve with yogurt or milk, or 1 of the following:

1 egg—beaten and cooked in, or boiled or poached and served on top of the oatmeal

1 tablespoon yogurt and honey

1 tablespoon old fashioned peanut butter

2 tablespoons sesame seeds

1 teaspoon butter

1 one-inch cube of cheese

Basic gravy (see chapter two)

Fruit—raisins or any fresh, frozen or canned (dietetic or with honey) fruit

My favorite topping is a pinch of salt and a teaspoon of butter or cream cheese.

2. Coddled Eggs

Place 4 eggs in cold water; add 1 tablespoon vinegar. Bring to a boil, turn off heat and let sit for five minutes. Eat with whole grain toast (4 slices) and any fruit or juice.

A dash of parmesan cheese does wonders.

3. Cornmeal pancakes

Mix 2½ cups whole wheat flour, 1½ cups corn-meal and 4 teaspoons baking powder. Add ¼ tea-spoon of salt and ¼ cup of honey.

Add 1/8 cup butter and 1/8 cup corn oil.

Beat 2 eggs and fold in.

Add ½ cup cream and beat well.

Cook on hot griddle.

Serve with fruit syrup (below) or just with cream cheese.

Fruit syrup

Add ¼ cup honey to 1 cup of any fresh or frozen fruit. Bring to a boil.

Whisk in 1 tablespoon guar gum and 1 table-spoon pectin. Boil two to five minutes.

4. Millet

To 2 cups boiling water, add ½ cup millet and simmer for 20 minutes. (Can be cooked overnight in a slow cooker.)

Serve with yogurt or milk or in any of the ways suggested for serving oatmeal in recipe #1.

Millet needs seasoning. Butter, parmesan, cream cheese, salt, etc. make the difference.

5. Rye pancakes

In a mixing bowl, crack 2 eggs. Add:
1 cup milk
½ cup rye flour
1 tablespoon baking powder
½ cup honey
Beat for 3 minutes and bake on a hot griddle.

Serve with fruit syrup (see page 61), or eat with a tiny bit of butter and fruit juice.

For variety, try putting the pancakes on a greased cookie sheet and baking at 400° for 10-12 minutes.

6. Berry pudding cake

Blenderize:

2 cups apple juice

1 cup yogurt

2 eggs

1 tablespoon guar gum

2 tablespoons arrowroot flour

Turn off blender. Mix in 2 cups of any berry (blackberries are my favorite) and 1 cup rolled oats.

Pour into greased custard cups and bake at 375° for 20 to 25 minutes.

Serve with milk or herb tea.

Can be cooked the night before and eaten cold.

7. Toast with peanut butter

Spread 3 tablespoons old fashioned peanut butter on four slices of whole grain toast.

Serve with fruit or juice.

For something different, spread the peanut butter on the bread before toasting it, then toast for 10 minutes in a 400° oven.

8. Omelet

In a mixing bowl, beat:

4 eggs

½ cup milk

Pour into cast iron pan with 1 teaspoon melted butter and 1 teaspoon oil.

Cook over medium heat without stirring for about 20 minutes.

Eggs will rise like a souffle.

Serve with 4 slices whole grain toast and fruit.

Eggs don't need salt. But they are great with sliced tomatoes sprinkled with dill weed.

9. Cream of rice

Thoroughly grind ⅔ cup of rice in blender while you bring 2 cups of water to a boil.

(Or buy cream of rice.)

Whisk in the ground rice.

Simmer 20 minutes.

Serve with yogurt or milk or in any of the ways suggested for serving oatmeal in recipe #1.

Cream of rice needs flavoring—at the very least, a little butter and salt.

10. Oatmeal waffles

In blender, beat 2 eggs for 5 minutes. Add:

1 cup milk
1 tablespoon oil
1 tablespoon butter
2 teaspoons baking powder
1 tablespoon honey
1 cup rolled oats

Pour about ¼ of the mixture on to a waffle iron and bake.

Blenderize the mixture again before baking each waffle.

Serve waffles with fruit syrup (see page 61).

Or just eat like cookies with butter or cream cheese.

11. Barley grits

To 2 cups boiling water, whisk in ⅔ cup barley grits.

Simmer for 20 minutes.

Serve in one of the ways suggested for serving oatmeal in recipe #1.

12. Scrapple

To 2 cups boiling water, whisk in:

1 tablespoon gelatin

⅔ cup corn meal

3 oz. of *any* ground meat scraps (including liver)

Add 1 teaspoon grated onion or ½ teaspoon onion powder plus:

¼ teaspoon thyme and/or sage

A dash of pepper and nutmeg

Stir over low heat 10 to 15 minutes. Pour into a buttered loaf pan. When cooled to room temperature, place overnight in the refrigerator.

For breakfast, slice, dip in flour and grill slowly.

Serve plain or with one of the suggestions for serving oatmeal (see recipe #1).

Scrapple is wonderful with scrambled eggs and sliced tomatoes—something special when inlaws visit. Actually, my inlaws introduced me to this delicious meal.

13. Codfish cakes

Beat together:
½ cup cod fish
1 egg
3 medium sized boiled potatoes (or ½ cup rolled oats or bread crumbs). If you wish, add:
1 teaspoon onion
½ teaspoon mustard
Worcestershire, A-1 or Heinz 57 sauce
Shape into patties and grill.
Serve with 2 to 4 slices whole grain toast.
Try it with horseradish!

14. Muselei

To 1 tablespoon oil in a medium warm cast iron pan, add:
2 cups rolled oats
2 tablespoons almonds
½ cup raisins
½ cup chopped dried apples
Stir fry for five minutes.
Serve in one of the ways suggested for serving oatmeal in recipe #1.
Yogurt and apple juice over muselei are super.

15. Potato pancakes

Wash and then grate in a food processor enough potatoes to provide 2 cups.

Grate 1 onion into the potatoes.

Beat well 3 eggs and add to the potato and onion mixture, mixing well.

Mix 2 tablespoons whole wheat flour and 1 teaspoon baking powder. Add to potato mixture and mix well.

Grill as small pancakes.

Serve while freshly cooked with:

Butter and salt.

Cream cheese or sour cream.

Applesauce, any fruit sauce, or cheese.

Milk or herb tea.

16. Popcorn

Make popcorn in the usual way.

Serve with yogurt, cheese, milk, peanut butter, or fruit.

Or mix up a syrup of 1 tablespoon butter boiled about 3 minutes with ¼ cup molasses, stirring well, and pour over the popcorn.

Popcorn is a neat and unusual cereal.

17. Muffins

Heat oven to 400°.
Beat briefly:
½ cup whole wheat flour
1 tablespoon honey
1 heaping teaspoon baking powder
2 eggs
1 tablespoon oil
¼ cup milk
Pour into buttered cast iron muffin pans and bake for 25 minutes.
Serve as is or with any of the following:
1 egg—soft boiled, poached or scrambled
Yogurt and fruit
Milk
1 tablespoon old fashioned peanut butter
Fruit or juice
1 ounce of cheese

18. Corn grits

To 2 cups boiling water, whisk in ⅔ cup corn grits. Simmer 10 to 15 minutes.
Serve in one of the ways suggested for oatmeal.
Excellent with a little parmesan cheese.

19. Granola

Best fixed the evening before.
Mix in a large bowl:
3⅔ cups rolled oats
¼ cup bran
¼ cup wheat germ
¼ cup sesame seeds
¼ cup sunflower seeds
⅓ cup cashews
⅓ cup almonds
⅓ cup coconut
Mix separately in a blender:
⅓ cup oil
¼ cup molasses and ⅓ cup honey (or ½ cup of either molasses or honey)

Stir liquid ingredients into granola. Spread on cookie sheet and bake at 350° for 20 to 30 minutes, stirring several times.

Serve in the morning as you would oatmeal.

For quick granola, prepared in the morning:
Pour the oil into a heated cast iron pan. Whisk in the dry ingredients and pour the molasses and honey over the granola while stirring briskly.

Whisk frequently while "grilling" for about 10 minutes.

20. Apple pancakes

Beat 2 eggs, add ¼ cup sour milk or yogurt.
Whisk in:

⅓ cup whole wheat flour

1 teaspoon of honey

1/8 teaspoon of salt

¼ cup sour cream or yogurt

Saute 1 sliced apple with 1 teaspoon safflower oil in the bottom of a baking dish or cast iron skillet.

Pour batter over apples and bake at 450° for 20 minutes.

Sprinkle pancakes with 1 tablespoon honey, ⅓ teaspoon ground cinnamon, and 2 teaspoons butter. Return to oven for 3 to 5 minutes. Remove and slice.

Meanwhile, mix the juice of 1 lemon with 2 tablespoons honey. Serve over top of pancakes.

21. English muffins

Toast purchased whole wheat English muffins (or whole wheat pita bread) with cheese.

Serve with fruit or juice, milk or herb tea.

Another great quickie!

22. Baked eggs

Baked eggs are a special treat. They can be placed in the oven with only two or three minutes work and bake while you shower and dress. When you are ready, so is a great breakfast!

Break 1 or 2 eggs into a buttered custard cup and bake at 350° for 10 to 15 minutes.

Spread whole grain bread with butter and toast in oven along with the eggs.

Serve with juice, fruit, milk and/or herb tea.

Sprinkle eggs with cheese for added taste.

23. Rice

Add 1 cup rice to 3 cups boiling water.

Stir in rice and bring back to a boil.

Cover and cook on *low* heat for 15 to 20 minutes, until all the water is absorbed.

Serve in one of the ways suggested for serving oatmeal in recipe #1, or with 2 ounces of any kind of fish, chicken, sausage, or any meat.

Try a pinch of curry and salt with raisins or sliced banana.

24. Peanut butter muffins

Blenderize lightly:

⅔ cup whole grain flour

½ tablespoon baking powder

¼ cup old fashioned peanut butter

2 tablespoons honey

1 tablespoon oil

You may add 1 egg. After blenderizing, add ½ cup of any nuts, sesame seeds, or raisins.

Fill the cups in a well-buttered cast iron muffin pan not more than ⅔ full.

Bake at 350° about 20 minutes.

Serve with milk, juice, herb tea. For a brunch, add any meat, cheese, or fruit salad.

This makes a wonderfully simple breakfast. Mix in five minutes and bake while you shower and dress.

25. Yogurt

Mix a variety of sliced fresh fruits and a few chopped nuts with yogurt for a great, quick breakfast. If you need bulk, add a couple of slices of whole grain toast.

26. Cheese Souffle

Heat oven to 350° while you blenderize:
1 teaspoon butter
1 tablespoon whole wheat flour
½ cup milk
2 to 3 ounces of cheese
2 or 3 eggs
Pour equal amounts into buttered custard cups.
Bake 15 to 20 minutes.
Serve with baked buttered toast, flat bread or
English muffins, fruit or juice, milk and herb tea.
Spread butter on bread and bake alongside the souffles.

27. Kedgeree

Any smoked fish will do—even canned salmon or tuna.
Beat 2 eggs with ¼ cup milk.
Pour over 1 cup leftover rice.
Gently mix in ½ cup flaked fish with 1 teaspoon
parsley. Sprinkle with a pinch of curry powder,
nutmeg and pepper.
Place in buttered pan and bake in 350° oven for
15 minutes, or stir fry in a cast iron pan for 10 to
15 minutes.
Serve with tomato slices or touch of horseradish.

74

28. Baked French toast

Any whole grain bread is suitable. Even better made with whole wheat English muffins or bagels!

Beat 2 eggs and ½ cup of milk.

Pour into a flat dish or pan and thoroughly soak 4 slices of bread.

Place in oiled or buttered pan.

Pour any leftover egg mixture over the bread and bake at 350° for 15 to 20 minutes.

While it bakes, shower and dress.

Serve as is or with honey, fruit syrup, jam or yogurt with honey or fruit. Accompany with fruit juice, milk or herb tea.

29. Cream of whole wheat

Whisk ⅔ cup cream of wheat into 2 cups of boiling water. Simmer 10 to 15 minutes.

Serve with yogurt or milk, or in one of the ways suggested for serving oatmeal in recipe #1.

As with most hot cereals, butter and a touch of salt are great on cream of wheat.

30. Baked peasant bread

Heat oven to 350° while you mix in the blender:

¼ cup kidney beans or garbanzos

1 egg

¼ cup bean liquid from kidney beans or garbanzos

½ cup corn meal

1 teaspoon chili powder

¼ teaspoon cumin

2 ounces of cheese

½ onion

½ clove garlic

1½ teaspoons oil

1 teaspoon sesame seeds

Pour into an oiled or buttered cast iron pan and
bake 15-20 minutes while you shower and dress.

Serve with sliced tomatoes, bell pepper, parsley
or tomato or V-8 juice.

If you like it hot, add a small bit of jalapeño pepper.

31. Egg McHome

Butter a flat, oven-proof dish. Place in it 4 slices of whole grain bread or English muffins.

Place on top of each slice of bread or muffin 1 slice of Canadian bacon and 1 egg.

Add cheese on top, if desired.

Bake at 350° for 20 minutes while you shower and dress.

Excellent served with tomato, celery, pimento, green pepper, tomato or any vegetable juice.

32. Oatmeal cakes

Mix well 1 egg with 1 cup water or milk.
Whisk in:

1 ½ cups rolled oats

1 teaspoon oil

¼ teaspoon baking powder

Drop large spoonfuls onto hot griddle or oiled cast iron skillet. Brown on both sides.

Serve plain or with honey, fruit syrup, yogurt or cheese. Fruit, juice, milk or herb tea round out a filling breakfast.

33. Forever young food

Blenderize:
2 tablespoons peanut butter
2 tablespoons honey
1 tablespoon oil
1 tablespoon almonds
1 tablespoon sunflower seeds
1 tablespoon coconut
1 tablespoon sesame seeds
1 tablespoon lemon juice
1 tablespoon chia seeds
Serve over dry rolled oats or whole grain toast. As always, you may serve with fruits, yogurt, juice, milk or herb tea.

Make a bigger batch; it keeps weeks in a closed jar, refrigerated.

34. Liver pudding

Blenderize or grind 3 ounces of liver.

Mix with 2 cups cooked rice, ½ chopped onion and 1 beaten egg.

Bake in an oiled or buttered cast iron pan 10 to 15 minutes at 350°.

Serve with fruit or juice and herb tea.

35. Tofu and scrambled eggs

Beat 2 eggs and whisk in 3 ounces of Tofu.

Mix in ½ cup mushrooms. If desired, add a dash of pepper or soy sauce.

Place in a lightly oiled cast iron pan over medium to low heat and cook slowly. Or bake at 350° for 20 minutes.

Serve with fruit or juice and herb tea.

Parmesan cheese on top is great.

36. Cheese muffins

Blenderize:

1 egg

½ cup milk

2 ounces of cheese

1 tablespoon oil.

Pour into a mixing bowl. Whisk in ⅔ cup whole grain flour (or ⅓ cup each rolled oats and wheat flour) and 2 teaspoons baking powder.

Pour into buttered cast iron muffin pan and bake at 350° for 20 to 25 minutes, while you shower and dress.

Serve with fruit or juice and herb tea.

37. Baked hominy

Blenderize 1 egg and ½ cup milk. Pour into greased cast iron skillet.

Mix in 1½ cups canned hominy and bake at 375° for 12 to 15 minutes.

Serve with sliced tomato, fruit, or juice, and herb tea.

38. Rice pudding

Blenderize:
2 eggs
½ cup milk
2 tablespoons honey
¼ teaspoon cinnamon

Mix with 1½ cups cooked rice and place in 2 greased custard cups.

Bake at 350° for 20 to 25 minutes, while you shower and dress.

Excellent with raisins and apples.

39. Cheese toast

Place 4 slices of whole grain toast on a cookie sheet and cover with thin slices of cheese.

Broil or toast in toaster oven.

Serve with tomato, vegetable juice or herb tea.

A *great quickie breakfast!*

40. Rolled rye cereal

Boil 2 cups water and whisk in ⅔ cup rolled rye.

Simmer on low heat for 5 minutes, stirring occasionally. Cover and let sit 2 to 5 minutes.

Serve with yogurt or milk, or in one of the ways suggested for serving oatmeal in recipe #1.

41. Baked scrambled eggs

Beat or blenderize 4 eggs and ½ cup milk.

Pour into 2 custard cups and bake at 350° for 20 to 25 minutes. Serve with whole grain toast, fruit or juice and herb tea.

Almost anything can be added to the eggs before baking: cheese, tomatoes, peppers, onions, meat, fish, etc.

42. Salmon cakes

Beat 1 egg. Mix with:
½ cup rolled oats
1 cup salmon
Place mixture in 2 custard cups and bake at 350° for 20 minutes.

Serve as is or with sliced tomato, vegetable juice and herb tea.

43. Cheese grits

Whisk ⅔ cup corn grits into 2 cups boiling water.

Turn heat to low and simmer, stirring occasionally. After 5 minutes, whisk in 2 ounces of grated cheese. Turn off heat and let sit 5 to 10 minutes, while you shower or dress.

Eat as is or with milk, if you prefer porridge.

44. Salmon and mushrooms

Saute 1 cup salmon with 1 4-ounce can of mushrooms and 1 diced onion.

Serve with a bagel and cream cheese.

45. Eggs and potato omelet

Wash and slice thinly, or cut into small cubes:
4 medium-sized potatoes
Blenderize:
4 eggs
1 onion
½ clove garlic
Mix thoroughly with the potatoes and pour into a lightly greased cast iron skillet.
Bake 25 to 30 minutes at 350°.
Serve as is or with sliced tomatoes, peppers, vegetable juice, fruit or fruit juice.
Try mixing in chopped sausage or other meat before baking for a truly hearty breakfast.

46. Cracked wheat cereal

Boil 2 cups of water.
Whisk in ⅔ cup cracked wheat.
Turn heat to low and simmer 5 minutes, stirring occasionally. Cover and let sit 2 to 5 minutes.
Serve with yogurt or milk or in any of the ways suggested for serving oatmeal in recipe #1.

47. Bagels

Baking bagels is fun, but takes an hour of time, so I suggest buying whole wheat bagels at the food co-op or a health food store.

Slice through two bagels so the hole is intact. Toast.

Spread with cream cheese and add slices of lox for a gourmet quickie breakfast. Serve with fruit, fruit juice, and herb tea.

For brunch, add baked scrambled eggs.

48. Peanut butter corn sticks

Mix in the blender:

½ cup whole grain flour

½ cup cornmeal

½ cup milk

1 egg

3 tablespoons peanut butter

⅓ cup honey

Pour into buttered corn stick pans (or muffin pans) and bake at 375° for 15 to 20 minutes while you shower and dress.

Serve as is or with a small piece of cheese, milk, fruit or juice.

49. Quiche

A *gourmet pan omelet with a crust. Quiche can be made in hundreds of different ways.*

Blenderize:

2 eggs

4 ounces cream or yogurt

3 ounces of cheese (Swiss or Farmer's)

1 onion

For a spinach quiche, add ½ package frozen spinach.

Pour over 4 slices of whole grain bread in a slightly greased pan.

Bake at 375° for 20 to 25 minutes.

Serve as is. For brunch, make the spinach quiche and serve with sliced tomato, carrot, celery and fruit salad.

50. Humus Toast #1

Mix 2 tablespoons humus and 2 tablespoons peanut butter. Spread on whole grain toast, English muffins or pita. Great with fruit or alfalfa sprouts, carrot juice, V-8 juice, milk or herb tea.

Humus is a great chick pea (garbanzo) food, high in protein and lower in fat than peanuts.

51. Spoon bread

Blenderize:
1 egg
1 cup cornmeal
1 teaspoon honey
1 cup milk or buttermilk
1 teaspoon baking powder
Pour into greased cast iron skillet and bake at 375° for 20 to 25 minutes, while you shower and dress—or do your morning limbering.

Serve as is, accompanied by vegetables or fruit.

For variety, add to the batter: chopped green or hot peppers, onions, grated cheese, ham, tuna or salmon.

52. Hamburger

Place 2 to 3 ounces of lean ground meat, shaped into patties, in a cast iron skillet with ¼ cup water.

Cook on high heat until water is half evaporated.

Turn heat to low and turn hamburgers.

Meanwhile, toast two pieces of pita.

Serve meat in pita with any of the following: cheese, lettuce, pickles, alfalfa sprouts and tomato sauce.

53. Granola bars

Mix in a bowl:
1 cup rolled oats
1 cup whole grain flour
1 egg, beaten
¼ cup wheat germ
½ cup milk or yogurt
2 tablespoons oil
½ cup raisins
½ cup honey or molasses
½ cup chopped nuts (walnuts, pecans, almonds)
¼ cup sesame seeds
¼ cup chopped dried fruits (apricots, peaches, and/or apples)

Pour the thick batter into a greased cast iron skillet or pan. Bake at 350° for 20 to 25 minutes.

Cut into squares while warm.

Great as is or with milk, fresh fruit or herb tea.

These granola bars may be stored up to two weeks in foil or Handi-wrap, or frozen and defrosted in a toaster oven.

54. Cranberry muffins

Mix in blender:
1 cup whole grain flour
1 ½ teaspoons baking powder
¼ cup honey
1 egg
½ cup milk
1 tablespoon oil
After blending, add 3/8 cup of cranberries mixed with 2 tablespoons of honey.

Pour into a well-buttered muffin pan and bake for 20 minutes at 350°.

These are rich and don't need butter. Hot out of the pan and served with milk, juice or herb tea, they make a superb quick breakfast. For brunch, add a small bit of meat or cheese and a fresh fruit salad.

For a nice touch, add a tablespoon of frozen orange juice concentrate or grated orange peel while blending.

55. Hot sausage tart

Blenderize:

1 egg

½ cup tofu

1 cup yogurt

½ teaspoon curry powder

½ onion

Place whole grain flat bread in greased cast iron skillet. Slice sausage over the flat bread and pour blender mix over the sausage.

Bake at 375° for 20 to 25 minutes.

Excellent with sliced tomatoes sprinkled with dill.

56. Apple nut pie

Blenderize:

2 eggs

½ cup of honey

1 teaspoon baking powder

½ apple (or chop and fold in)

Fold in ¼ cup whole grain flour, ¼ cup chopped nuts and 1/8 teaspoon vanilla extract.

Pour into a greased cast iron skillet.

Bake at 350° for 25 minutes.

Serve with milk or yogurt, fruit, juice or herb tea.

57. Bran muffins

Blenderize for 2 to 3 minutes:
1 egg
¼ cup honey or molasses
⅔ cup milk or yogurt
1 tablespoon oil
1½ teaspoons baking powder
Fold in ⅔ cup bran. Add:
⅔ cup whole grain flour
½ cup chopped nuts
¼ cup raisins
Pour into a greased cast iron muffin pan.
Bake at 350° for 20 to 25 minutes.
Serve with fruit, juice, milk or herb tea.
These muffins are a meal in themselves. For a hearty brunch, add eggs, meat, and yogurt with fruit.

58. Sweet potato cereal

Bake a medium to large sweet potato the night before, placing it in a timed oven before you go to bed. In the morning, slice it and serve with milk, just like cereal. Add raisins and chopped apple, or yogurt with honey, if desired.

59. Tofu quiche

This is one quiche "real men" do eat!
Blenderize ¼ cup tofu with:
1 tablespoon arrowroot flour
1 heaping tablespoon soy flour
¼ teaspoon guar gum
1½ teaspoons honey
1½ teaspoons garlic powder
dash of black pepper
1 tablespoon sesame seeds
1 tablespoon oil
Place 4 slices whole grain bread in a greased cast iron skillet.

On top of bread, place 1 cup or so of any vegetable of your choice—sliced zucchini, thawed frozen spinach, chopped onion, etc.

Pour the blender mix over the bread and bake at 375° for 25 minutes.

Serve with herb tea, fruit or juice.

60. Tuna fish cakes

Mix together:
6 ounces tuna
1 cup rolled oats
1 beaten egg
A pinch of pepper
½ chopped onion
Make into patties or place in custard cups or muffin pan. Bake at 350° for 20 minutes, while you shower and dress.

Serve alone, or with toast or English muffin, fruit, juice or herb tea.

61. Baked apple

Wash, core and slice 2 apples.
Mix together:
1 cup rolled oats
¼ cup raisins
¼ cup yogurt
¼ cup molasses or honey
Spread mixture over apples in a greased cast iron pan. Bake at 350° for 20 minutes.

Serve with milk or herb tea. Or top with yogurt, cinnamon and honey.

92

62. Steak

Start your day today with the meat of the day. Any steak will do, but the leaner the better.

Trim fat from 2 pieces of steak (3 or 4 ounces) and place in a cast iron skillet. Add 1 cup water.

Cook on high temperature. When water is half evaporated, turn steak. As water evaporates, turn to low heat. The steak will cook in 5 to 10 minutes.

Serve with whole grain toast or popcorn, sliced tomato or a salad, tomato or V-8 juice.

A *great way to start the day.*

63. Pumpkin pudding

Blenderize ½ cup of any grain. Add:

1 cup cooked pumpkin, squash, sweet potatoes or carrots

1 tablespoon arrowroot flour

2 eggs

1 cup milk

3 tablespoons honey or molasses—use only 1½ tablespoons for sweet potatoes or squash

Pour into custard cups and bake at 375° for 20-25 minutes.

Serve with milk, juice, fruit or herb teas.

64. Beans and rice

Start brown rice as described in Chapter 2. As the rice cooks, begin preparing the beans.

To 2 cups of any beans (canned or cooked overnight in a slow cooker), add:

2 tablespoons tomato sauce or ¼ cup tomatoes

1 small chopped onion

1 tablespoon peanut butter mixed in ¼ cup hot water

1 bay leaf

Cover and simmer 15 to 20 minutes.

Serve over brown rice.

65. Cream of rye

Whisk ⅔ cup rye flour into 2¾ cups of boiling water, whisking briefly until boiling resumes. Turn to low heat and simmer 10 minutes.

Add ½ cup raisins or chopped dates.

Serve with yogurt or milk, or in any of the ways suggested for serving oatmeal in recipe #1.

66. 12-grain cereal

Start the night before. Place in a slow cooker 4 tablespoons each of: sesame seeds, wheat, rye, barley, millet, rice, triticale, soy grits, corn grits or cornmeal, rolled oats, buckwheat, and peanut butter. Add 8 cups of water and cook on medium overnight.

In the morning, move the pot to the stove and whisk for 2 minutes on high heat.

Serve with milk or yogurt, or in any of the ways suggested for serving oatmeal in recipe #1.

Save leftover cereal by pouring into a greased loaf pan and refrigerating when cool. It can then be sliced and grilled for another neat breakfast.

67. 12-grain pancakes

Slice leftover 12-grain cereal, dip in flour or arrowroot flour, and grill on medium heat.

Serve plain or with yogurt, hot fruit syrup (see page 61), butter, cheese, milk, fruit, juice, etc.

68. Oven pancake souffle

Heat oven to 425°. In a mixing bowl, whisk:
½ cup whole grain flour
½ cup milk
2 eggs
1/8 teaspoon nutmeg
Blend in 2 tablespoons melted butter, pour mixture into cast iron skillet and bake for 15 to 20 minutes. Meanwhile, simmer the juice of 1 lemon mixed with 4 tablespoons of honey.

Serve pancake with hot lemon sauce, fruit, juice and milk or herb tea.

69. Pan bread

Blenderize:
1 cup whole grains or flour
2 tablespoons arrowroot flour
⅓ cup corn meal
3 tablespoons soy flour
Add 1 cup water and 1 egg; blend.

Pour into greased cast iron skillet and bake at 375° for 15 to 20 minutes.

Sliced tomatoes or fruit complement this dish well.

70. 10-grain pancakes

Blenderize thoroughly 2 tablespoons each of: rye, rice, wheat, corn, buckwheat, soy grits, rolled oats, triticale, millet, and barley. Add:

1½ cups water or milk

1½ teaspoons baking powder

1½ teaspoons oil

Brown both sides on a hot griddle and serve with butter or hot fruit syrup (see page 61).

71. Banana nut treat

Blenderize:

3 tablespoons peanut butter

1 banana

1 teaspoon arrowroot flour

⅓ cup water

Pour over 4 slices of whole grain bread in a greased pan.

Bake at 350° for 15 to 20 minutes.

Serve with fruit, hot fruit syrup, applesauce, milk, juice or herb tea.

73. Oat pan bread

Blenderize:

1 tablespoon sesame seeds
1 tablespoon soy flour
2 cups rolled oats
1 cup water
1½ teaspoons baking powder
2 tablespoons honey
1½ teaspoons oil

Pour into a greased pan and bake at 375° for 20 to 25 minutes.

Serve as is or with butter, hot fruit sauce, cheese, meat, milk, juice or herb tea.

73. Humus toast #2

Blenderize:

1 cup cooked or canned chick peas
2 tablespoons sesame seeds
½ cup milk or water

Serve over whole grain toast with fruit, juice, milk or herb tea.

74. Apple porridge

This is best cooked overnight, but it can be prepared in 15 minutes in the morning.

Place in a slow cooker:

2 cups rolled oats

2 cups applesauce

½ cup raisins

¼ cup sesame and/or sunflower seeds

½ cup chopped nuts

1 cup water

Cook on low heat overnight.

Serve with milk or cream in the morning.

75. Rice cereal

Starting the night before, place in a slow cooker:

1 cup brown rice

4 cups water

Cook on medium overnight.

In the morning, whisk the cereal while you increase the heat to near boiling. (This takes only about 2 minutes.)

Serve with yogurt or milk, or in any of the ways suggested for serving oatmeal in recipe #1.

76. Breakfast cookies

Blenderize:

¼ cup barley

¼ cup millet

¼ cup rye

¼ cup oats

1 tablespoon arrowroot flour

1 tablespoon lecithin granules

¼ cup nuts

Pour into a bowl and add:

1 tablespoon oil

¼ cup molasses or honey

1 beaten egg

½ cup raisins

Mix well. Drop by tablespoons onto a greased cookie sheet and bake at 350° about 15 minutes.

Serve with fruit, juice, milk or herb tea.

Can be cooked the night before while you're cleaning up from dinner.

77. Breakfast dessert

Blenderize:

½ cup hot apple juice

1 package gelatin

1 teaspoon guar gum

2 tablespoons honey

Add:

1 egg

1 cup yogurt

1 cup of fruit of your choice

Pour into sherbet or custard dishes and place in freezer for 15 to 25 minutes, while you dress.

Eat with peanut butter toast for a filling meal.

78. Corn-oat cereal

Whisk into 6 cups boiling water:

1 cup rolled oats

1 cup corn grits

2 eggs

Turn to low heat and simmer about 15 minutes.

Serve with milk or yogurt, or in any of the ways suggested for serving oatmeal in recipe #1.

Pour leftovers into custard cups, cool and refrigerate for use the following day.

79. Corn custard

Using yesterday's leftover cereal, top with:
2 tablespoons yogurt
2 to 3 tablespoons of fruit of your choice—applesauce, pears or peaches are excellent
1 tablespoon nuts
Bake at 400° for 15 to 20 minutes. Serve as is or
with raisins, dates or dried peaches.

80. Pork chops

Place 2 lean pork chops or pork tenderloin in a
cast iron pan with 1 cup water. Bake at 400° for
25 to 30 minutes while you shower and dress.
Serve with whole grain toast, applesauce and
milk or herb tea.

81. Tapioca

Soak 2 tablespoons tapioca in 2 cups of milk for
15 minutes, then boil 15 minutes while whisking.
Serve in a dish with sliced bananas or other fruit
and honey.

82. Rice pudding

Use up leftover cooked rice with this recipe!
Blenderize:
1 cup of milk
2 eggs
2 cups cooked rice
2 tablespoons honey
a dash of cinnamon, cloves and nutmeg
Pour into custard cups and add a tablespoon of raisins to each cup.

Cook at 350° for 15 minutes.

83. Hot dogs in a blanket

Lay 4 hot dogs (all meat or vegetarian) in a slightly greased corn stick pan. Blenderize:
1 cup corn meal or corn grits
1 cup water
1½ teaspoons oil
1 teaspoon baking powder
Pour the mixture over the hot dogs and bake at 375° for 15 to 20 minutes.

Serve with a dash of mustard or horseradish, cranberry sauce and herb tea.

84. Spanish rice

Another overnight dish. Spend 5 minutes putting it together the night before and it will be ready when you waken.

Place in a slow cooker:

½ cup garbanzos

1 cup rice

4 cups water

½ chopped onion

½ chopped green pepper or pimento

1 cup tomato sauce

¼ teaspoon garlic powder

a dash of curry powder or chili powder

1 tablespoon soy flour

Cook overnight at medium heat.

85. Millet and soy porridge

This cooks overnight, or in 20 minutes in the morning.

Add 1 cup millet and 2 tablespoons soy flour to 4 cups of water in a slow cooker.

Cook overnight on medium heat.

Transfer to stove in morning and whisk in 1 egg or 2 tablespoons of peanut butter.

Serve with yogurt or milk, or in any of the ways suggested for serving oatmeal in recipe #1.

86. Curried rye

It's your choice: overnight or 20 minutes in the morning.
Place in a slow cooker:

1 cup whole rye

3 cups water

½ onion

½ teaspoon curry powder

2 tablespoons peanut butter or soy grits

¼ cup raisins

1 tablespoon unsweetened coconut

1/8 teaspoon Lite-salt

Cook overnight on medium heat. Serve with applesauce or sliced fruit of any type. Yogurt and fruit are also good with this dish.

87. Cheese & sausage omelet

Brown 4 to 6 ounces of lean sausage in a cast iron skillet. Pour off grease.

Meanwhile, mix together: ½ cup milk, 2 eggs, ½ cup grated sharp cheddar cheese, 1/8 teaspoon dry mustard, and 2 slices crumbled whole grain bread.

Pour over sausage, stir, and bake 20 minutes at 425°. Serve with tomatoes, fruit, milk or herb tea.

88. Banana bread

Blenderize 2 cups rolled oats. Add:
1 cup apple juice
1 banana, very ripe
2 tablespoons honey
2 tablespoons wheat germ
¼ cup nuts
a dash of cinnamon and nutmeg
1 egg
1½ teaspoons baking powder
1 tablespoon arrowroot flour
Pour into greased custard cups and bake at 375° for 20 to 25 minutes.
A meal in itself. Serve with herb tea.
You can fix this the night before and toast it for breakfast.

89. Buckwheat groats

Bring 2½ cups of water to a boil and whisk in 1 cup buckwheat groats. Simmer for 25 minutes.
Serve with yogurt or milk, or in any of the ways suggested for serving oatmeal in recipe #1.
Raisins or dates and cream cheese go well with buckwheat.

90. Peach custard pie

Grease pie pan with oil or butter and sprinkle liberally with wheat germ or a mixture of wheat germ and rolled oats. Blenderize:

1 cup milk

2 cups of peaches

2 eggs

1 tablespoon arrowroot flour

1 teaspoon guar gum

Pour into pie pan and bake at 375° for 20 to 25 minutes. Serve with herb tea.

And you can fix it the night before, if you choose.

91. Gumbo

This one *must* be cooked overnight. Place in a slow cooker:

1 cup dry lima beans

4 cups water

1 cup rice

1 cup tomato sauce

1 cup okra

1/8 teaspoon pepper (or chili, tabasco or curry)

Cook on medium heat overnight. For extra taste, add 1 ounce of ham or a ham bone.

92. Cheese grits

This dish can be fixed in the morning, but it is best if started the night before, in a slow cooker.

Place 1 cup corn grits with 3 cups of water in slow cooker and cook overnight on medium heat.

The next morning, whisk in 2 ounces of grated cheese and let stand until served.

Excellent with vegetable juice, tomatoes and fruit.

93. Granola a la Lawrence

Mix together:
1 cup rolled oats
½ cup wheat germ
¼ cup *each* of soya flour, wheat bran, dried skim milk, sunflower seeds, sesame seeds, chopped nuts, coconut and raisins.

Blend 1 cup honey and 1 tablespoon oil. Stir into dry mixture thoroughly and bake on cookie sheets at 375° for about 15 minutes.

Serve with warm milk and apple or grape juice.

Make a double or triple batch and store in a closed jar for a quick cold cereal breakfast.

LUNCHES

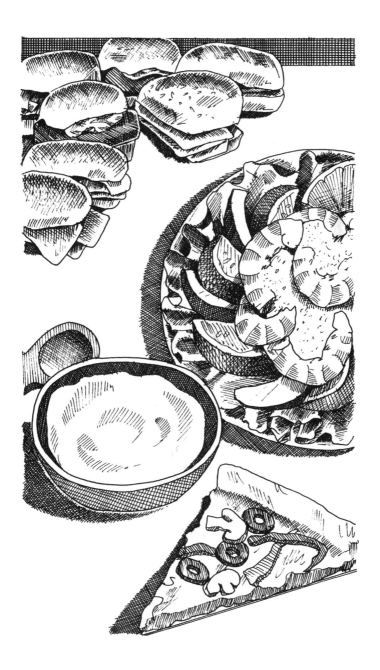

Ideally, the *biggest* meal of the day should be eaten at midday, but it might make you sleepy. And in most American families, the evening meal is the family's time together. Still, lunch is an important meal and deserves thoughtful attention.

I have divided the lunch recipes into three categories: salads, soups and sandwiches. Each menu is sufficient for a meal, but you may also want to mix and match.

SALADS

Salads make a wonderful meal *if* you serve an excellent whole grain bread with them. Hearty rolls and thick sliced bread are my favorites.

Americans do not eat enough greens—and certainly not a wide variety. Consider all the ''greens'' available to us:

Head lettuce	Leaf lettuce
Romaine lettuce	Endive
Kale	Chard
Spinach	Rape
Celery	Cucumbers
Green peppers	Cabbage
Broccoli	Kohlrabi
Cauliflower	Parsley
Corn salad	Basil
(you may have to grow it)	Fennel
Scallions	Green onions

111

Any and all of these greens can be mixed. And all can be prepared in the morning for serving at lunch.

There are many dressings you can make for salads. Recipes for the more well-known ones can be easily obtained. The Nearly Famous Deli in Springfield, Missouri, one of my favorite gourmet restaurants, has generously shared with me it's great salad dressing. They use romaine lettuce but the dressing is equally good on any greens.

Nearly Famous salad dressing

Very gourmet.

Toss greens with sliced pimento and add a few sliced, canned artichoke hearts.

Sprinkle generously with Parmesan cheese.

Just before serving, add a mixture of 2 parts oil (I prefer safflower oil) to 1 part Heinz® wine vinegar. The Heinz *does* taste best.

1. Dilled tomato yogurt

Slice tomato and cucumber over 8 to 12 ounces of yogurt. Sprinkle generously with dried dill weed.

Serve with whole wheat pita bread, flat bread or whole wheat English muffins.

2. Chick pea delight

Grate or chop in a food processor:

2 carrots

1 turnip

3 radishes

Mix with 1½ cups canned chick peas. Sprinkle with curry powder. Serve on lettuce with whole grain bread.

3. Carrots plus

Grate or shred 2 carrots, a fourth of a cabbage and a half of a rutabaga. Serve with 8 ounces of cottage cheese (not creamed) and sprinkle with wheat germ. Serve with your favorite bread.

4. Rice salad

Plan ahead! This salad requires leftover rice.
Mix together: 1 cup chick peas, 1 cup cooked rice, chopped green pepper, celery, onions, olives, 1 teaspoon oil, pepper, dill and rosemary.

5. Tabouli

Chop 2 tomatoes, 2 small (or 1 medium) onion and one cucumber. Mix with:
½ cup wheat germ
¼ cup rolled oats
2 tablespoons lemon juice
1 tablespoon oil
No bread needed. Serve on greens, if desired.

6. Avocado

Slice a large avocado in half, remove seed.
Top with 4 ounces of cottage cheese, tofu or yogurt and a cup of grapes or berries.

7. Slaw and wheat

Chop or grate:
one-half of a cabbage
3 radishes
⅓ cup nuts of your choice
¼ cup raisins
Mix with 2 tablespoons of mayonnaise and serve in a pita or with any whole grain bread.

8. Yogurt dip

Grate or break into small chunks cauliflower, green peppers, carrots and broccoli. Toss with 2 tablespoons lemon juice mixed with 8 ounces of yogurt. Season with pepper, thyme and basil.

Serve with bread, over rolled oats, or over cooked brown rice.

9. Chick pea

Mix 1½ cups of chick peas, sliced red onions, chopped celery, and 1 tablespoon lemon juice.
Serve on lettuce with pita.

10. Apple-grape salad

Grate or chop two apples. Add:
1/3 cup chopped nuts
1 cup grapes
1 tablespoon lemon juice
Serve on lettuce, kale, chard or spinach with cold cooked rye, rice, or a whole grain bread.

11. Orange-banana-pineapple

Chop and mix:
1 orange
1 banana
1 small can unsweetened pineapple
3 tablespoons unsweetened coconut
Serve with cottage cheese, yogurt or tofu, and bread.

12. Sweet potato

Slice a cold baked sweet potato and serve with raisins, sliced orange, crushed unsweetened pineapple and greens.

13. Asparagus

I *love raw asparagus, but you may prefer canned or cold steamed asparagus.*

Place 2 cups asparagus spears and 2 table-spoons mayonnaise on lettuce. Serve with cold rice or rye or boiled potatoes.

14. Bean salad

Mix 2 cups of cooked or canned beans (lima, kidney, navy or green beans) with chopped onion, green pepper, lemon juice and tarragon.

Serve on greens or with a hearty bread.

15. Chokes and potatoes

Boil 4 potatoes in advance, let cool, and slice. Combine with 2 sliced Jerusalem artichokes, 2 sliced hard boiled eggs, 2 tablespoons yogurt mixed with 1 teaspoon lemon juice and tarragon.

Jerusalem artichokes are a real gourmet treat. They taste like water chestnuts but are less expensive and very low in calories.

16. Spinach salad

Boil 4 small potatoes in advance, let cool.

On a large bed of spinach, place the potatoes, 2 sliced hard boiled eggs, chopped celery, kohlrabi and carrot, 1 tablespoon lemon juice and 4 tablespoons yogurt or cottage cheese.

17. Cabbage

Serve this salad with cold boiled potatoes and sliced, nitrate-free frankfurters.

Grate:

2 to 3 cups of cabbage

1 bell pepper

1 Bermuda onion

Place in glass or pottery dish. Boil:

3 tablespoons honey

¼ cup cider vinegar

2 tablespoons oil

¼ teaspoon dry mustard

¼ teaspoon celery seed

Pour over the salad, cover, and place in the freezer for 10 minutes or refrigerate.

This salad keeps two to three weeks.

18. Chick pea tabouli

Chop fine:
2 tomatoes
1 onion or 2 scallions
1 green pepper
¼ cup parsley
¼ cup fresh mint
Add: 2 tablespoons lemon juice, 1 tablespoon oil, pepper and tarragon.

Mix with ½ cup wheat germ and 1½ cups chick peas. Serve on lettuce, spinach, kale or chard.

19. Macaroni and vegies

Grate 2 carrots, 1 cucumber, 2 radishes and 1 green pepper.

Mix with 2 cups cold cooked whole wheat or soya wheat macaroni, 1 tablespoon sesame seeds, 2 tablespoons yogurt, 1 teaspoon lemon juice, pepper, rosemary and thyme.

Serve with greens.

Whole grain pasta tastes better and offers much more nutritionally. It cooks the same as other pasta—place in boiling water for about 5 to 10 minutes, drain.

20. Tomato aspic

Blenderize:
2 cups tomato juice, canned tomatoes or 2 fresh tomatoes
2 stalks of celery
1 tablespoon dill seeds
½ teaspoon paprika
2 tablespoons lemon juice
1 heaping tablespoon guar gum
1 package of gelatin
Pour into a custard dish and chill. Serve with greens and cold boiled eggs, cold boiled potatoes or macaroni.

21. Potato salad

Slice 4 cold potatoes and mix with:
¼ cup parsley
1 green pepper and 1 Bermuda onion
2 hard boiled eggs
Serve with mayonnaise and tofu or yogurt on greens.

Plan ahead: boil a dozen medium potatoes (30 to 45 minutes) to have on hand for this and other recipes. They will keep in a covered dish in the refrigerator for 2 to 3 weeks.

22. Turnip salad

Chop turnips, cabbage, radishes and carrots. Mix with 2 tablespoons sesame seeds, ¼ teaspoon celery seeds, ⅓ cup chopped nuts and 2 tablespoons lemon juice.

Serve with pita and greens.

Just as good with rutabaga instead of turnips.

23. Rice legume

Plan ahead: cook rice or rye for dinner the night before, so you'll have leftovers to use in this salad.

Mix 2 cups cold cooked rice or rye with 1 cup cold cooked green peas, 1 grated carrot, 6 chopped olives and 1 Bermuda onion.

Serve with 1 tablespoon mayonnaise and 1/8 teaspoon curry powder.

24. Tuna salad

Mix 6 ounces canned (water packed) tuna fish with 1 tablespoon mayonnaise and serve on top of mixed greens, with flat bread.

25. Potato and chick peas

Mix 4 cold boiled potatoes (chopped or sliced) with 2 cups chick peas, chopped onion and parsley. Serve on greens.

Or use 2 cups cold cooked rice instead of potatoes.

26. Rice pudding salad

Mix 2 cups cold rice with 2 sliced bananas, plus:
¼ cup chopped nuts
1 tablespoon sesame seeds
¼ cup raisins

Cooked rice also stores well, up to 10 days in a closed container in a refrigerator.

27. Cabbage and beets

Slice or chop: 1 cup beets, 1 cup cabbage, 2 carrots and ¼ cup nuts.

Serve with greens, cold potatoes, macaroni, rice or pita.

28. Mixed cold vegies

Mix zucchini, okra, lima beans, green beans, chick peas and kidney beans. Top with alfalfa sprouts. Serve with a hearty bread or popcorn.

The okra and lima beans need to be steamed 8 to 10 minutes; the zucchini and green beans may be raw or steamed. The chick peas and kidney beans can be canned; if you used dried beans, they will require several hours of cooking. Be sure all cooked vegies are cold before using.

29. 4-bean salad

Mix together cold green beans, kidney or navy beans, chick peas, green peas and chopped or sliced onion. Pour over the mixture 2 tablespoons oil and 1 tablespoon lemon juice or vinegar.

Serve on lettuce or other greens.

The green beans can be raw or cooked; the rest should be canned.

30. Okra-tomato aspic

Blenderize:
1 cup cooked okra
2 cups tomatoes
2 tablespoons guar gum
1¾ teaspoons curry powder
Pour into custard cups and chill.
Fix this one while you're getting dinner and it will be ready for lunch the next day.

31. Mixed greens with salmon

Mix 6 ounces of canned salmon with 1 table-spoon mayonnaise, basil and dill weed.
Serve on mixed greens.
Wonderful with sourdough French bread.

SOUPS

Soups are meals in themselves. They are good with French bread, English muffins, flat bread or whole wheat crackers. Most soups can be fixed with five or ten minutes preparation time, but they are usually best if prepared in advance and then cooked slowly. *Plan ahead*!

1. Indiana bean soup

Place in a slow cooker with 1 quart water:
⅔ lb. dried lima beans
1 onion and 1 apple
1 ham bone
1/6 teaspoon savory
1 teaspoon parsley
Cook on medium heat 8 to 20 hours. Twenty minutes before serving, place 1½ cups sauerkraut in a pot with 4 sliced frankfurters on top. Bring to a boil and simmer for 15 to 20 minutes.

Remove ham bone and blenderize soup. If too thick, add chicken soup or milk.

Put sauerkraut and franks in two bowls and ladle soup over it. Serve with flat bread, whole grain crackers or buns.

The slow cooker comes into its own with this gourmet soup.

2. French onion

Slice or chop 2 medium onions and saute in 1 tablespoon oil in a cast iron skillet. Sprinkle with 1 tablespoon flour or arrowroot and whisk for 1 minute. Add:

½ teaspoon Worcestershire sauce

½ clove minced garlic

1 can of beef consomme plus ½ can water or an equal amount of beef stock

Bring to a boil. Pour soup into 2 serving dishes and place whole wheat English muffin on top of each. Sprinkle generously with grated cheese of your choice and broil for 1 to 2 minutes.

Can also be fixed in slow cooker: saute onion right in the pot and cook on low overnight or at least 4 hours on high.

3. Navy bean soup

Fry 1 ounce ground pork sausage with 1 cup chopped onion and ½ clove minced garlic in a cast iron pan. Pour off fat.

Blenderize: ½ cup dry navy beans, 3 cups water and 1 tomato. Add to sausage, bring to near boil and simmer 20 to 25 minutes.

Even better cooked in a slow cooker.

4. Cream of asparagus

Heat 1 tablespoon oil in a skillet. Whisk in 2 tablespoons flour or arrowroot flour. Add 1 cup milk or cream and turn heat to low.

In a separate pot, cook 1 package frozen asparagus with 1 cup water. Blenderize, then add to cream mixture and simmer.

In another skillet, saute croutons made from two English muffins or 3 slices whole grain bread (sliced into eighths) in 1 teaspoon butter, 1 teaspoon oil and ½ minced clove garlic.

Dip croutons into anchovy paste or liver pate (1 tablespoon is enough for all the croutons). Serve soup in 2 bowls, with croutons on top.

The anchovy paste or pate adds a great touch of class.

5. Lemon rice soup

Cook for 6 to 20 hours on medium in a slow cooker: 1½ pints water, 1 medium chopped onion, 1 ounce of any meat and 1 cup rice.

Blenderize 2 eggs with 1/8 teaspoon thyme or rosemary and the juice of one-half lemon.

Stir into the soup and cook 10 minutes on high.

If you use cooked rice, you can fix this in 15-20 minutes.

127

6. Gazpacho

Blenderize:
1 cup tomato juice and 1 cup consomme
1 stalk celery and 1 clove garlic
1 tomato
juice of one-half lemon
1 tablespoon oil
2 medium onions
½ green pepper
a dash of hot pepper or Tabasco
2 tablespoons egg white or ½ cup cooked or canned chick peas
Pour into 2 dishes with ice cubes. Serve cold with popcorn.

7. Creamed almond soup

Blenderize with 3 cups water:
½ cup almonds
1 tablespoon arrowroot
1 tablespoon oil
1 cup cooked rice
1 teaspoon soy sauce
Bring to near boil. Simmer five minutes.
For an extra treat, serve with cheese toast.

128

8. Garlic soup

Blenderize in 2 cups of water:

1 ounce beef

1 package gelatin

2 cloves of garlic

1 egg

2 tablespoons sesame seeds

1/8 teaspoon pepper

½ cup cooked chick peas or lima beans

Heat 1 tablespoon oil in a skillet and whisk in 1 tablespoon flour or arrowroot flour.

Pour blender mix into skillet and bring to a boil. Simmer for 3 to 5 minutes.

You may want to avoid friends a few days, but this is even better than onion soup. Try cooking it in a slow cooker, too.

9. Tuna bisque

Blenderize: 1 ounce ground beef, 2 tomatoes, a 6-oz. can of tuna, 1 package gelatin, 2 cups water (or 1 cup milk or cream), ½ cup yogurt, 1 tablespoon parsley, 1 onion and 1/8 teaspoon pepper.

Pour into a pot and bring to a boil. Simmer for 3 to 5 minutes.

Or skip the blender and cook it in a slow cooker overnight.

10. Oyster soup

Brown 2 ounces chicken, minced, in 2 table-spoons oil in a large cast iron skillet. Add:
3 cups water
½ cup yogurt
1/8 teaspoon pepper
2 tablespoons arrowroot flour
1 stalk celery
1 bay leaf
½ pint oysters
Bring to a boil and then simmer on low for 15 to 20 minutes. Serve with popcorn.
This soup is best fixed just before serving it.

11. Pumpkin soup

Blenderize: 1 ounce meat, 1 package gelatin, 1 tablespoon arrowroot flour, 3 cups water, 1½ cups yogurt, 1½ cups canned or cooked pumpkin or squash and 1 tablespoon honey or molasses.
Bring to near boil and simmer 10 to 15 minutes.
Sprinkle with nutmeg, cinnamon or cloves.
Also good cooked overnight in the slow cooker.

12. Mint pea soup

Cook 6 to 20 hours on medium in a slow cooker:
½ cup split peas
1 ounce meat
1 package gelatin
4 cups water
½ clove garlic, minced
When done, add 4 sprigs mint, 1 teaspoon parsley and a pinch of tarragon and thyme. Blenderize and serve either hot or over ice cubes.

You can fix this speedily by blenderizing the peas, meat, gelatin, garlic and water before cooking. Add mint at end.

13. Potato chowder

Blenderize with 3 cups of water:
3 medium potatoes, sliced, and 1 onion
1 cup of corn
½ clove garlic
½ cup yogurt
1 tablespoon oil
1 tablespoon arrowroot flour
Bring to near boil and simmer 15 to 20 minutes.

Add fish, clams or chicken for a heartier meal. Also lends itself to slow cooking. Same work, but you must plan ahead.

14. Spinach soup

Blenderize with 3 cups of water:
1 ounce of meat
1 package gelatin
1 package thawed frozen spinach
1 onion and 1 clove garlic
1 tablespoon oil
1 tablespoon arrowroot flour
Pour into a pot and add 1 cup cooked or canned chick peas, lima beans, navy beans or soybeans.
Heat to near boil and simmer 15 to 20 minutes.

15. Instant curried chicken

Blenderize with 3 cups of water:
1 to 2 ounces of cooked chicken
1 package gelatin
1 teaspoon curry powder
½ cup yogurt
1 teaspoon honey
one-half of a lemon
1 tablespoon unsweetened coconut
1 tablespoon almonds
Pour over ice cubes and serve cold, or heat to near boil and serve hot.

16. Fish chowder

Blenderize with 3 cups of water:
1 cup corn and ½ cup yogurt
1 clove garlic and 1 onion
1 tablespoon oil
4 to 6 ounces of boneless fish
1 tablespoon arrowroot
Pour into a pot and bring just to a boil. Lower heat and simmer 15 to 20 minutes.
Add 1/8 teaspoon nutmeg on top after serving.
Can also be cooked in the slow cooker.

17. Vegetable soup

Cook 6 to 20 hours on medium in a slow cooker:
⅓ cup dry beans of any kind
2 stalks chopped celery
1 tablespoon oil
1 chopped onion and 2 chopped carrots
3 cups of water
2 tomatoes or 1 cup canned tomatoes
½ cup each of millet and barley
1/8 teaspoon each of basil, savory, tarragon, rosemary and thyme
Or *blenderize and cook in 20 minutes.*

18. Okra soup

Blenderize ½ package frozen okra, 1 cup of tomatoes, 1 celery stalk and 1 onion. Pour into a pot with 4 ounces of hamburger and 2 cups water. Bring to a near boil and simmer for 15 minutes.

19. Potato soup

Blenderize: 3 cups of water, 3 medium sliced potatoes, 1 onion, 1 stalk of celery, ½ cup yogurt, 1 package gelatin, 1/8 teaspoon pepper, 1 tablespoon arrowroot and ½ cup canned or cooked chick peas, lima beans, soy beans or navy beans. Bring to a near boil and simmer 15 minutes.

20. Kohlrabi soup

Saute 1 ounce ground beef and 1 onion, then blenderize with 3 cups water, 1 package gelatin, 1 stalk celery, ½ cup cooked garbanzoes and 2 chopped kohlrabi. (You may omit sauteeing.)

Bring to near boil and simmer for 15 minutes.

All soups on this page can also be fixed in a slow cooker.

21. Kale or chard soup

Saute 1 ounce ground beef with ½ clove garlic and 1 chopped onion. Blenderize:

1 package gelatin

3 cups flour

1 tablespoon arrowroot flour

½ cup yogurt

Add to beef mixture in pan, bring to near boil and simmer for 15 minutes.

At serving time, stir in 2 cups chopped kale or chard—or spinach or watercress.

Best fixed this quick way.

22. Rutabaga soup

Cook 6 to 20 hours in a slow cooker:

1 chopped onion

1 ounce beef

1 package gelatin

3 cups water

1 cup frozen green beans or ⅓ cup dried green peas (or any dried bean)

one-half medium rutabaga, chopped

Or blenderize and cook from scratch in 20 minutes.

23. Bean soup

Cook 6 to 20 hours on medium in a slow cooker:
4 cups water
½ cup rice (or rye, millet or barley)
1 chopped onion
1 stalk chopped celery
1 tablespoon oil
½ teaspoon salt
½ cup mixed dried beans—navy, kidney, soy, chick, lima, lentils, green or yellow peas or pinto
Or *blenderize and cook from scratch in 20 minutes.*

24. Cream of mushroom

Saute 1 chopped onion, 1 stalk chopped celery and ½ clove garlic in 1 tablespoon oil. Blenderize:
1 cup cooked garbanzoes
3 cups water
1 tablespoon arrowroot flour
1 cup mushrooms
Add to onion mixture and heat to near boil. Simmer 10 to 15 minutes.
Can also be fixed in a slow cooker.

25. Beef barley soup

Cook 6 hours on medium, or up to 20 hours on low, in a slow cooker: 3 cups of water, 4 to 6 ounces of beef stew or ground beef, 1 tablespoon oil, 1 chopped onion, 2 tomatoes, 1 stalk chopped celery and ½ cup barley.

It's best this way, but you could blenderize the ingredients and cook them in 20 minutes.

26. Bouillabaise

Place in a slow cooker with 3 cups water:
1 chopped clove garlic
1 onion and 1 carrot
1 cup tomatoes
1 package gelatin
1 ounce ground beef
1/8 teaspoon thyme
½ teaspoon parsley

Cook on low heat for 6 to 8 hours. Then add: 6 frozen shrimp, 2 ounces fresh or frozen fish, and 1 lobster tail or 3 crab legs.

Bring soup to a boil and cook at a low boil for 20 minutes.

Any fish is great—a mixture is ideal!

27. Black bean soup

Cook 6 to 20 hours on medium in a slow cooker:
⅔ cup black beans
4 cups water
1 tablespoon oil
1 chopped onion
½ clove minced garlic
1 stalk chopped celery
a pinch of pepper
½ cup rice or millet
1 ounce of meat
Blenderize or whisk briskly when cooked. As you serve it, mix in 2 tablespoons lemon juice and chopped hard-boiled egg.

Or blenderize and cook from scratch in 20 minutes.

28. Cream of cauliflower

Saute 1 chopped onion in 1 tablespoon oil.

Blenderize: 3 cups water, 1 ounce of beef, 1 package of gelatin, 1 stalk celery, one-half head of cauliflower and 1 tablespoon arrowroot.

Add mixture to onion and bring to near boil, then simmer for 15 to 20 minutes.

This soup can also be slow cooked.

29. Creamed cabbage soup

Blenderize with 3 cups of water:
2 cups chopped cabbage
1 onion
1 tablespoon oil
¼ teaspoon each of thyme and tarragon
½ cup cooked beans (soy, navy, lima or chick)
Bring to a near boil and simmer 15 minutes.
Best fixed this quick way.

30. Vichyssoise

Blenderize with 3 cups of water:
3 onions
3 medium potatoes
1 tablespoon oil
½ cup cooked chick peas
1 ounce beef
1 package gelatin
a pinch each of sage, basil and dill weed
Bring to near boil and simmer 15 to 20 minutes.
Serve very cold. Hot, it's just potato soup; cold,
it is vichyssoise!

If you prefer to use the slow cooker, cook the potatoes whole and blenderize at the end.

31. Chicken rice soup

Place in a slow cooker with 4 cups water:
2 pieces of chicken
⅔ cup chopped celery
1 chopped onion
1 cup rice
Cook 6 to 8 hours on medium or up to 24 hours on low. Or blenderize and cook in 20 minutes.

32. Lentil soup

Chop 1 carrot, 1 stalk celery, 2 medium potatoes, 2 tomatoes and 1 onion.

Place in slow cooker with 4 cups of water:
1 cup dry lentils
1 ounce meat
1 bay leaf
1 cup rice, barley or millet.

Cook 6 to 20 hours at medium heat. At serving time, add 1 teaspoon lemon juice.

Or *blenderize and cook in 20 minutes.*

33. Minestrone

Place in a slow cooker:

4 cups water

1 cup whole wheat or soy wheat macaroni

1 tablespoon oil

1 chopped onion

1 bay leaf

1/8 teaspoon oregano

1 to 2 cups total of green beans, tomatoes, summer squash, carrots, celery and parsley

Cook 6 hours at medium or up to 20 hours on low heat.

Or you could blenderize everything but the pasta, cook the vegies for 20 minutes and the pasta for 5 to 10 minutes separately, drain the pasta, and then add the two together at the end.

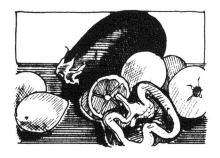

SANDWICHES

The bread makes the difference in a good sandwich. *Real* whole grain breads have a texture and a taste that far outshine "white" bread. My grandfather called store-bought bread "wasp's nest." That's an insult to the wasp. So-called "enriched flour" is deficient in 28 essential nutrients, especially vitamin B_6. If the package doesn't say 100 percent whole wheat, it isn't! Fiber deficiency is another problem in unwholesome white bread (and puns on "wholesome" don't make up the difference). No gourmet would use white bread except an occasional loaf of sourdough French bread. Even with sourdough, whole wheat is superior.

If you haven't tried Durkee's® special sauce, it's a real treat—one of the few store-bought mixes that is superb. Try it on most of the sandwiches. You can make your own substitute by mixing mayonnaise, mustard and horseradish, but it won't taste any better than Durkee's.

Major Grey's Mango Chutney® is another gourmet condiment that goes well with many sandwiches, especially the meat ones.

And if you can find some homemade chow-chow relish, don't pass it up. It's a great relish for sandwiches and equally good in salads.

Other good companions for sandwiches, served on the side, are a few almonds, pecans, walnuts, a little *fresh* coconut, fresh or dried fruit, or a couple of canned artichoke hearts or hearts of palm.

Sandwich fillings

1. Old fashioned peanut butter. Serve with 1 stalk of celery or fresh fruit.

2. Cottage cheese and tomato. Spread cottage cheese on bread, add sliced tomato, alfalfa sprouts and olives.

3. Cheese. Spread bread with mayonnaise and add sliced cheese and lettuce, spinach, kale or chard.

4. Pate. Saute 4 ounces of chicken livers and 1 chopped onion for 5 minutes in 1 tablespoon oil.

Blenderize with ½ cup cooked garbanzoes, 1/8 teaspoon ginger, 1 teaspoon soy sauce and 1/8 teaspoon dry mustard.

Spread on bread. Serve with lettuce or sliced Bermuda onion.

This pate can be made more gourmet with an ounce of dry sherry. And it will keep a week or two in a closed container in the refrigerator.

143

5. Salmon loaf. Spread bread with mayonnaise or horseradish. Place a slice of salmon loaf on bread and top with greens, green peppers, etc.

Plan ahead. This is an easy sandwich to fix using leftover salmon loaf from dinner #66.

6. Bean. Blenderize or grind 1 cup cooked beans. Spread on bread and add sliced onions and greens. Canned beans do nicely.

7. Roast beef. Spread bread with horseradish and add roast beef, greens and beets.

Children prefer to skip the beets.

Plan ahead: use roast beef from a "weekend joint."

8. Pimento cheese. Mash together 3 ounces of cheese, 1 tablespoon mayonnaise and 1 pimento. Spread on bread. Serve with celery and carrot sticks.

Real Wisconsin sharp cheddar is best.

9. Turkey. Top bread with mayonnaise, turkey, greens, celery, green pepper and sprouts.

Use leftover turkey from an earlier dinner. Or as a special treat, use smoked sliced turkey, available at better grocers.

10. Almond-sesame. Grind together in blender ½ cup almonds, 2 tablespoons pecans or peanuts and 2 tablespoons sesame seeds.

Mix with 1 tablespoon mayonnaise and spread on bread. Serve with fresh fruit.

11. Pizza. Blenderize or grind: 1 cup cooked or canned pinto or navy beans (or chick peas), 1 tomato, 1 onion, one-fourth of a green pepper, ½ clove garlic, 1/8 teaspoon oregano and 1/8 teaspoon rosemary.

Spread on sandwich and add generous amounts of grated parmesan or romano cheese. Grill, toast or eat cold.

12. Salmon. Spread bread with mayonnaise, add canned salmon. Serve with greens or sprouts.

13. Egg. Mash 3 soft boiled eggs with 1 teaspoon horseradish, 1 teaspoon mayonnaise and 1 chopped pickle. Serve with celery, greens, sprouts, chow-chow, etc.

14. Banana nut. Spread low-fat cream cheese on bread. Mash together 2 bananas and 2 tablespoons chopped nuts.

15. Avocado. Mash together: 1 avocado, 1 banana, 2 teaspoons honey and 1 tablespoon chopped nuts. Spread on bread and add sprouts.

16. Tuna. Mix tuna with mayonnaise, 1 chopped carrot and 1 stalk celery. Spread on bread; top with greens.

17. Reuben. Spread horseradish thinly on bread. Add well drained sauerkraut, sliced frankfurters and swiss cheese. Grill or eat cold.

18. Rutabaga. Mash together 1 cup cooked rutabaga, 1 cup garbanzoes, 1 stalk chopped celery and one-half of an onion. Spread on bread and serve with greens.

Plan ahead: cook the rutabaga the night before. Use the slow cooker or a low heat (250°) oven overnight.

19. Fish. Spread bread with mustard or horseradish, sprouts and greens.

Any fish will do. If you don't have leftovers, or didn't cook some in advance, use canned salmon. Your cat will love you.

20. Chili beans. Grind or blenderize: 1 cup canned or cooked kidney beans, 1 small onion, 1 tomato, 1 stalk celery and 1 slice green pepper.

Sprinkle with red pepper and serve in pita bread.

21. Sardines. Place sardines packed in mustard on pumpernickel. Add a few slices of onion and green pepper. Wonderful with boiled egg on the side.

Sardines (and salmon) are high in EPA (not the Environmental Protection Agency, but a type of oil that's good for your arteries)!

22. Humus.   Blenderize: 4 tablespoons dry sesame seeds, 1 tablespoon oil, 2 cups cooked chick peas, ½ clove garlic and one-half of a lemon.

Spread on bread, saving half for another lunch. Serve with greens, celery, beets and sprouts.

An especially nutritious and tasty spread. Canned chick peas are widely available and taste even better this way than in salads. A pinch of salt may be desirable.

23. Peanut butter & banana.   Mash together 2 bananas and 2 tablespoons peanut butter.

Serve with raisins, dates or greens.

24. Frankfurter.   Slice frankfurters.   Spread bread with horseradish.   Lay franks on bread. Serve with sprouts, greens and green pepper.

Canned franks can be used straight from the can or jar. Bake any others at 450° for 10 minutes before using.

25. Turnip & nut. Mash together 1 cup cooked turnips or rutabaga and 2 tablespoons peanut butter or 4 tablespoons almonds or cashews. Spread on bread and serve with greens or sprouts.

Son Brock says, ''Good luck!'' But don't knock it if you haven't tried it!

26. Beet. Blenderize or grind: 1 cup cooked beets, 1 cup garbanzoes, 1 onion and one-fourth of a lemon. Spread on bread. Serve with sprouts or greens.

Plan ahead: boil beets on simmer overnight. Use canned garbanzoes (chick peas).

27. Brats and kraut. Place well-drained kraut on bread and add cooked bratwurst. Excellent cold or hot.

Real brats are rarely available outside Wisconsin and Ohio, but any sausage can be used. Knockwurst is excellent. Brats can be boiled in beer for about 15 minutes or baked in an oven at 450° for about 12 minutes.

28. Cream cheese. Top cream cheese with dates, onions and chopped nuts. Serve with fresh fruit, especially bananas.

29. Ham. Spread bread with mustard or horseradish, add ham and a slice of cheese if desired. Serve with greens, sprouts and bell pepper.

Most store-bought ham is loaded with nitrates and salt. Unless you can find real ham, have this sandwich only occasionally.

Excellent with mango chutney or any relish.

30. Peanut butter & humus. Mix 2 tablespoons peanut butter with 4 tablespoons humus saved from sandwich recipe #22.

Serve on bread with sprouts or greens.

31. Sweet potato. Spread bread with a thin layer of low-fat cream cheese. Slice a sweet potato thickly. Add 1 slice unsweetened pineapple per sandwich plus a few raisins or dates.

Put the sweet potato in the oven the night before and cook all night at 250° or use a timed oven.

DINNERS

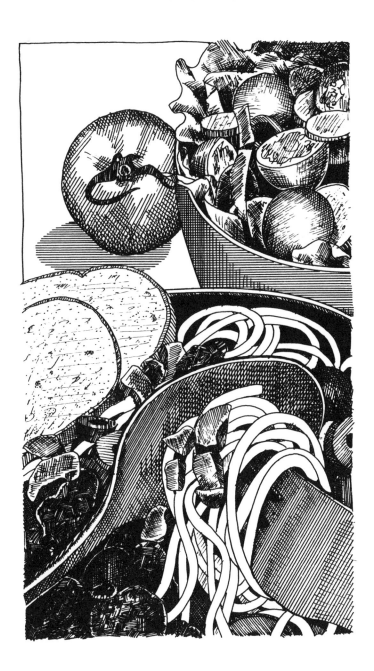

Dinner, the main meal for most people, can still be prepared quickly.

The key is to plan ahead. If you do, you can take advantage of such time-saving steps as preparing a slow-cooker meal or roasting pan dish late in the evening to be slow baked all day the following day and be ready for dinner that night. It may only take five minutes of work, but you have to plan ahead. I rarely spend more than 15 to 20 minutes of *work time* on any dinner.

Another trick is to fix two meals at the same time. If dinner is a quickie meal, start your lunch or breakfast for the following day while it's cooking. With minimal effort, you can have all the work done for it as well by the time you sit down for your evening meal.

The dinner menus offer a wide variety from light to very full meals. Most of the cooked vegetables will be used to accompany the dinners. Please look back at the list of vegie vegies—they're all super. Many are wonderful eaten raw with a mustard sauce (Durkee's again) or a sour cream, yogurt or buttermilk dip. All of them except lettuce can be steamed, and the French even do that. They call it lettuce fatigué, even though it's not—just left over! Once steamed, vegetables are best with a little butter. Most do well without any other seasoning. If you are not a purist and want to save on fat and calories, Butter Buds® give the right flavor. I have some reservations about their quality, but the amount used is so small that I occasionally use a sprinkle.

Most of the time, I steam vegies on top of rice or grains. When we're having vegies without rice, I use a simple steamer. It takes about 10 minutes from start to finish. And stir fry can be done even faster. Stir chopped vegies in 1 tablespoon oil and 2 tablespoons water at high heat; after two to three minutes, turn to simmer, cover and let the vegies cook briefly. The *total* time required is 5 to 10 minutes.

And don't forget baking. All the starchy vegies bake well. So does rice. And most beans and peas can be slow baked.

Herbs of all kinds enhance flavor and add subtle changes. Experiment! A touch of salt, a pinch of curry and a dash of dill weed, rosemary, thyme and even mint give you many choices.

Once you get into the Speedy Gourmet attitude, you will think of dozens of quick ways to alter and enhance flavor, not only with vegies but also with meats, grains, and legumes.

Speaking of meats, all red meats can be improved with a little red wine, rosé or beer. And marinating in wine, vinegar or lemon juice will tenderize and flavor the toughest of meat cuts. Fish and fowl are best cooked with a little dry white wine or lemon juice. But orange concentrate is also super. And for a real taste treat, cinnamon, nutmeg and/or cloves add delicate flavoring. Anise is good in meatballs.

In the recipe for meat loaf, I suggest wrapping it in cooking paper or parchment before placing it in the pressure cooker. *Real* cooking paper is patapar, available from the Heritage Store in Virginia Beach or gourmet shops. Cut a piece twice the size needed, butter lightly and place the loaf on it. Fold the edges together and pleat to close, making a well-closed package like a Christmas box. Turn it upside down to hold securely. If you don't have patapar, Reynolds® nylon cooking bags do substitute nicely. They are available in most grocery stores.

Fish is very nice prepared in cooking paper. It seals in the flavor.

Beef and lamb are best medium rare; the amino acids are more easily available for intestinal absorption. Pork and fowl need to be well done, but *not* charred. Fish is fine just good and hot; it requires little cooking. But it does require *some* cooking.

Dinners can almost always be made more elegant with quick biscuits, muffins or whole grain hard rolls. They can be prepared while the main dish is cooking. And any of the luncheon salads can be a basis for a small dinner salad, too.

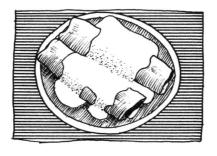

1. Henry's chicken

Mix in a paper bag 1/8 teaspoon each of thyme, paprika, onion salt, garlic salt, pepper and Lite Salt with ½ cup whole wheat flour and 2 tablespoons arrowroot flour.

Remove skin from 2 chicken legs or breasts and toss pieces in the bag, coating them evenly. Place in a slightly greased cast iron skillet.

Bake at 400° for 25 to 30 minutes or at 200° for 8 hours.

Prepare basic rice and cook on top of the steaming rice 2 sliced zucchini and 1 sliced onion.

Serve with greens.

For a real feast, serve with quick biscuits. See chapter 2 for recipes for both basic rice and quick biscuits.

2. Spinach casserole

Mix together 1 package cooked, drained spinach, 8 ounces of yogurt, 1 chopped onion and 2 cups cooked rice.

Place in a casserole with a dash of nutmeg on top and bake 20 minutes at 400°.

A great light dinner, but if it's too light for you, serve with whole grain bread topped with cheese and baked in the oven.

3. Eggplant with yogurt

Peel and slice 1 eggplant. Dip in flour and grill in minimally greased cast iron skillet.

Meanwhile, mix with 1 cup yogurt:

½ clove garlic, minced

¼ teaspoon dried mint or 1 sprig fresh mint

Serve over the eggplant with whole grain bread, greens and sprouts.

4. Sweet & sour scallops

Place 6 to 8 ounces of scallops in a greased cast iron skillet. Heat 1 tablespoon butter with 1 tablespoon oil. Whisk in:

2 tablespoons honey or molasses

1 tablespoon lemon juice

1 teaspoon dry mustard

a dash of pepper

Pour over scallops and broil 12 to 15 minutes.

Place in pressure cooker 3 medium potatoes, sliced, and cook at 15 pounds pressure for 10 minutes. Remove and whisk. Top with barbecue sauce.

Serve scallops and potatoes with greens, salad or cooked spinach.

5. Vegie stew

Place in slow cooker with 4 cups water:
½ cup soy beans
¼ cup each dried lima beans and lentils
¼ teaspoon sage
1/8 teaspoon each thyme, savory and basil
1 chopped onion and 1 chopped carrot
2 stalks chopped celery
½ cup wheat germ
1 clove minced garlic
1 cup grain of choice
1 tablespoon each soy sauce and brewer's yeast
Cook on medium 6 to 8 hours or low for 20 to 24 hours. Ten minutes before serving, grate 3 tablespoons cheese over top and turn to high.
Pickled peaches or crab apples go well with this.

6. Beef rib roast

Place a 1-rib roast (about 2 pounds) or a 1-pound sirloin tip in a roasting pan. Rub with minced garlic and sprinkle with pepper. Broil 12 minutes per side.

In pressure cooker, steam 3 medium potatoes, 2 onions and one-half a cabbage or 2 small kohlrabi.

7. Gourmet sole with grapes

Heat 2 tablespoons oil in a cast iron skillet. Add 1 teaspoon butter and one-half of an onion, chopped. Saute 1 minute.

Add 8 ounces filet of sole (or any fish) and 2 tablespoons dry white wine. Cover and simmer for 10 minutes. Remove fish and place on a platter in a warm oven.

Whisk in skillet:

¼ cup yogurt and 1 beaten egg

1 teaspoon honey and a dash of nutmeg

1 tablespoon arrowroot flour

Cook until thickened.

Add 1 cup of seedless green grapes. Pour entire sauce over fish and sprinkle with paprika.

Meanwhile, prepare basic rice, adding fresh—or a package of frozen—broccoli to steam on top.

Mix 2 teaspoons melted butter with the juice of a half lemon.

Serve rice and broccoli separately but pour lemon butter over both dishes. Serve fish, rice and broccoli with greens.

8. Potato & spinach casserole

Blenderize:
1 medium sliced potato and 1 onion
1 cup yogurt and 2 eggs
2 tablespoons soya flour
1 teaspoon soy sauce
½ pound fresh or 1 package frozen spinach
Pour into a greased cast iron skillet and bake at 400° for 25 minutes.

9. Baked beans and franks

Place 2 cups cooked or canned kidney, pinto or navy beans in a casserole dish.

Add 1 cup tomato sauce, 1 tablespoon molasses, ¼ teaspoon dry mustard, 1 chopped onion, and 2 sliced franks.

Bake at 400° for 20 minutes. Serve with cole slaw made by chopping or grating:
2 cups cabbage and 1 radish.

Mix with ½ teaspoon celery seed, 2 tablespoons mayonnaise, 1 teaspoon horseradish and 1 teaspoon mustard.

Serve with popcorn.

10. Pilaf with liver

Saute 1 chopped onion in 1 tablespoon oil at high heat in a cast iron pot. Add 1 cup *cracked* wheat or any cracked grain or brown rice. Saute on high for 2 to 3 minutes.

Add 2 cups boiling water plus:

1 package gelatin

1 tablespoon soy sauce

1/8 teaspoon each of cumin, rosemary, thyme, basil, oregano and tarragon

1 chopped carrot

Bake 25 minutes in a 400° oven.

While the pilaf is baking, saute 1 chopped onion in 1 tablespoon oil. Add 6 to 8 ounces sliced liver or chicken livers. Cook on medium heat.

Serve liver with chopped pimento over pilaf, accompanied with greens.

11. Pork chops

Heat ½ tablespoon oil in a pressure cooker. Add and brown 2 pork chops.

Add ½ cup water and 1 onion, cover and cook at 15 pounds pressure for 10 minutes.

Meanwhile, steam lima beans, corn and carrots.

12. Eggplant and humus

Cook 6 hours on medium heat in a slow cooker:
one-half peeled eggplant
⅔ cup chick peas
2 cups water
4 tablespoons sesame seeds
½ clove minced garlic
1 tablespoon oil
Blenderize and serve with sprouts and pita.

13. Tuna with pea sauce

Cook basic rice (or a rice, barley and millet mixture). When rice reaches bubble stage, steam 2 sliced carrots on top.

Blenderize ½ cup dried green peas and add:
1½ cups water
1 tablespoon arrowroot powder
Pour into a cast iron pan and bring to near boil. Stir in 1 can tuna and add ¼ teaspoon marjoram.

Cover and simmer until rice is done. Dish up rice with carrots on top, then ladle the tuna with pea sauce over that.

Serve with fresh or canned unsweetened pineapple.

14. Vegie burgers

Blenderize well ½ cup each of barley, chick peas and rolled oats. Add 2 cups water plus:
  ½ teaspoon paprika and 1 tablespoon soy sauce
  1/8 teaspoon pepper and one-half clove garlic
  1 stalk celery and one-half of an onion
Blenderize until smooth. Pour out of blender and shape into patties. Add rolled oats as needed for proper consistency. Grill in skillet or broil.

Serve with tomatoes, greens and pita.

Mango chutney adds zest to these burgers. This is an "adult" taste treat!

15. Soy bean chili

Mix in a slow cooker: 4 cups water, 1 cup soy beans, 1 cup any grain, 1 teaspoon chili powder, ¼ teaspoon each of red pepper and oregano, 1 clove minced garlic, 1 chopped onion, 1 jalapeño pepper, 4 chopped tomatoes or 1 cup tomato sauce and 1 tablespoon soy sauce.

Cook on medium heat 6 to 8 hours or on low for 20 to 24 hours. Serve with popcorn and greens.

If you don't like it hot, omit chili and red pepper but do use the jalapeño.

16. Pita bread pizza

Slice open 2 pieces pita bread. Spread with 8 tablespoons tomato paste or sauce. Sprinkle with basil, oregano, garlic powder, chopped onion, mushrooms, chopped nuts or sunflower seeds.

Add thin slices of Mozzarella cheese.

Bake at 400° for 8 to 10 minutes.

Top with alfalfa sprouts and serve.

If it wasn't so wonderful to eat, you might even want to use it as a modern centerpiece!

17. Wiener schnitzel

Roll in flour 2 slices of veal round, each ½ inch thick (4 ounces). Brown on both sides in a pressure cooker with ½ tablespoon oil.

Place veal on cooking rack and add ½ cup water.

Top each slice of veal with 1 slice of lemon. Surround with 6 small sliced potatoes. Cover and cook 15 minutes at 15 pounds pressure.

When pressure is down, open and add ¼ cup of sour cream. Heat 2 to 3 minutes.

Meanwhile, steam spinach. Serve with a small bit of butter and nutmeg.

Pumpernickel rolls with garlic butter add class.

18. Orange snapper

Place 6 to 8 ounces snapper (or other fish) in a greased cast iron skillet. Mix:

4 tablespoons frozen orange juice concentrate

1 tablespoon each of oil and melted butter

1 teaspoon soy sauce and a dash of pepper

Pour over fish. Broil 5 minutes. Turn, brush with sauce and broil another 5 minutes.

Cook basic rice, steaming sliced zucchini and brussels sprouts on top.

Serve rice and brussels sprouts with an orange butter sauce made by heating 1 tablespoon frozen orange juice and 1 teaspoon each butter and oil.

A tablespoon of Grand Marnier perks up the sauce.

19. Millet casserole

Mix with 3 cups boiling water:

1 cup millet

2 cups chopped vegies—onions, squash, kale, turnips or rutabagas, kohlrabi and carrots

2 tablespoons peanut butter

Pour into a cast iron skillet and bake at 400° for 25 minutes.

Dress it up with pickled peaches, dried apricots or raisins.

20. Meat loaf

Combine 4 ounces ground beef, 4 ounces ground pork, 1 egg, 1 minced onion, ½ cup chopped celery, 1 grated carrot, ¼ cup oatmeal and ½ teaspoon soy sauce. Form into a loaf and wrap snugly in patapar cooking paper.

Place in pressure cooker and add ½ cup water and 6 small potatoes or 2 larger sliced potatoes.

Cover and cook at 15 pounds pressure for 15 minutes. When cooked, place under broiler to brown. Serve with a salad.

21. Rice & peanuts

Cook ¾ cup brown rice.
Saute in 1 tablespoon oil:
1 chopped onion
½ cup chopped peanuts
2 tablespoons sesame seeds
½ cup chopped dried apricots or peaches
1/8 teaspoon cloves
½ teaspoon soy sauce and 1 teaspoon honey
Serve over the rice. Excellent with a fruit salad of oranges, bananas and coconut.

22. Mahi-Mahi

Place 8 ounces of Mahi-Mahi (or other fish) in a greased cast iron skillet. Heat together 1 tablespoon oil, 1 teaspoon butter and 1 tablespoon lemon juice. Pour over fish and broil 5 minutes.

Turn fish, brush with sauce and broil 5 minutes.

When done, top with grated almonds or macadamia nuts. Meanwhile:

Cook basic rice or a blend of rice, rye and millet. Steam green beans on top when rice reaches bubble stage.

Serve fish, rice and green beans with greens and orange or tangerine slices.

23. Eggplant stew

Place in a slow cooker with 2 cups water:
one-half of a peeled eggplant
½ cup chick peas
½ cup rice or millet
1 chopped onion and 2 tomatoes
1 tablespoon oil
¼ teaspoon pepper
Cook on medium heat 6 to 8 hours.
A *little garlic and cheese make this a real gourmet stew.*

24. Potato chili

Grate or grind 3 medium potatoes.

Pour into a greased skillet and add: 1 cup cooked or canned kidney beans, 1 cup tomato sauce or 2 cups tomatoes, 1 chopped onion, 1 clove minced garlic and 2 dashes of Tabasco or 1/8 teaspoon hot pepper.

Bake at 400° for 30 minutes.

Serve with greens.

Grated sharp cheddar can be added at serving time.

25. Swiss steak

Roll 2 pieces of round steak (4 ounces each) in flour. Heat pressure cooker and add ½ table-spoon oil. Brown meat on both sides. Add:

¼ cup diced celery

one-fourth of a green pepper, diced

1 minced onion

2 to 3 ounces tomato juice

Cover cooker and cook at 15 pounds pressure for 15 minutes.

Meanwhile, cook basic rice. At bubble stage, add sliced zucchini, cover and steam.

26. Beef Wellington

Pressure cook:

3 medium potatoes

2 carrots and 2 onions

2 small whole zucchini or artichokes

Preheat oven to 450°.

Rub 2 3-ounce tenderloins with 1 tablespoon cognac and sprinkle with pepper. Lay 2 strips bacon over the tenderloins and bake 15 minutes.

Remove steaks and set bacon aside for pate.

While steak cooks, saute on high for 5 minutes:

1 teaspoon each of butter and oil

½ clove minced garlic and 1 small onion

4 ounces of chicken livers

Blenderize bacon and liver mixture to make pate. Coat beef with pate and roll in a mixture of ½ cup rolled oats and 1 beaten egg.

Place in oven again for 5 minutes. Serve with the mixed vegetables.

If you fix the artichokes, make a sauce for them by blending together 1 tablespoon horseradish, ¼ teaspoon dry mustard, and 1 tablespoon vinegar or lemon juice.

As well as substituting artichokes for zucchini, try substituting asparagus for the carrots.

This is a banquet meal, excellent with any hearty bread and a mellow rosé wine.

27. Rice enchiladas

The *speedy* gourmet will use ready made tortillas!
Prepare basic rice. Have on hand cooked or canned pinto beans and tortillas.

To make tortillas, mix ½ cup wheat flour, ½ cup cornmeal, 1 teaspoon baking powder and 1½ teaspoons oil. Add enough cold water to make a stiff dough. Knead.

Put dough on floured board in heaping tablespoonfuls and flatten very thin. Cook on greased griddle.

Place 1 tablespoon cooked rice, 1 tablespoon pinto beans and 1 tablespoon chopped mix— onions, carrots, celery and green pepper—on each tortilla and fold over.

Grate cheese on top and broil 3 minutes.

28. Speedy fish

Place in a pressure cooker: ½ cup tomatoes, 1 bay leaf, 1 chopped onion, ½ tablespoon oil, 1/8 teaspoon pepper and 8 ounces of fish.

Cover and cook at 15 pounds pressure for 3 to 5 minutes. Serve with millet and steamed vegies.

A *touch of fresh lime juice is very gourmet.*

29. Spaghetti & meatballs #1

Mix together:

8 ounces ground beef (or half beef, half pork)

½ cup oatmeal

1/8 teaspoon pepper

1 small minced onion

1 egg

Make into small meatballs and brown in a pressure cooker with ½ tablespoon oil. Add 1 cup of tomatoes, one-half minced clove of garlic, 1 bay leaf and ½ cup red wine.

Close pressure cooker and cook 5 minutes at 15 pounds pressure. Meanwhile, bring 1 quart of water to a boil and add whole wheat or soy wheat spaghetti. Cook 5 to 10 minutes.

Serve with a mixed salad.

30. Millet & rice

Cook ¼ cup millet with ¼ cup brown rice, using basic recipe for rice.

Saute 1 chopped onion, ½ cup chopped almonds and ½ cup grated cheese in 1 tablespoon of oil.

Serve over millet and rice with a green salad.

31. Chicken

Cut 1 pound of chicken into serving pieces. Brown in a pressure cooker with 1 tablespoon oil.

Add 1 chopped carrot, 1 chopped onion, 1 cup tomatoes, ½ cup mushrooms and 1/8 teaspoon pepper. Cover and cook at 15 pounds pressure for 15 minutes.

Serve with brown rice and steamed vegetables.

32. Tofu and mixed vegies

Cook brown rice following basic recipe.

Place 1 cup tofu cut into 1-inch cubes and 2 tablespoons oil in a cast iron pan.

Chop and add to tofu:

2 stalks of celery

1 medium onion or small bunch of green onions

1 green pepper

one-half clove of garlic

Mix 2 tablespoons soy sauce and 1 tablespoon honey and add to tofu, along with 1 cup bean sprouts or alfalfa sprouts and 4 ounces fresh or canned mushrooms.

Simmer 2 to 4 minutes and serve over rice.

33. Pot roast

Rub a 1-pound roast with a mixture of ½ teaspoon each of ginger, cinnamon and nutmeg.

Brown roast in a pressure cooker with ½ teaspoon oil. Add:

2 small onions
1 tablespoon honey
¼ cup red wine
¼ cup water
2 bay leaves

Cover and cook at 15 pounds pressure for 25 minutes.

Meanwhile, prepare rice or a rice, rye and barley mixture. Steam cauliflower, broccoli, spinach or kale, as desired, on top of rice mixture.

34. Poached fish

Place in a pressure cooker with ½ cup water:

8 ounces of fish
1 chopped onion
1 teaspoon parsley and 1/8 teaspoon pepper
1 slice of lemon

Cook 3 minutes at 15 pounds pressure.
Serve with rice and steamed vegies.

173

35. Mixed beans & cole slaw

Mix together a total of 1½ cups of dried lima beans, chick peas, azuki beans, mung beans, pinto beans and black-eyed peas.

Add 3 cups of water and cook in a pressure cooker at 15 pounds pressure for 35 minutes.

Meanwhile, saute 1 chopped onion and ½ clove garlic in 1 tablespoon oil in a cast iron pan.

Whisk in 2 tablespoons arrowroot flour and add:

1 teaspoon curry powder

¼ teaspoon salt

1/8 teaspoon ginger powder

1½ cups milk

4 ounces tomato sauce

Simmer, then serve as a sauce for mixed beans.

To make cole slaw, chop and grate:

one-half of a small cabbage

2 carrots

1 beet

1 celery stalk

Mix in:

2 tablespoons chow-chow or chopped pickles

2 tablespoons mayonnaise

2 tablespoons mustard

Serve with bread.

Adding 1 cup creamed corn to mixed beans makes a good variation.

36. Stew

Heat pressure cooker. Brown 8 ounces of cubed stew meat, lamb, or lean pork in ½ tablespoon oil.

Add 2 cups green beans plus:

6 small potatoes

2 medium tomatoes

2 small carrots

½ cup water

Cover and cook at 15 pounds pressure for 10 minutes. Cool cooker and add a whisked mixture of 1 tablespoon arrowroot flour and 2 tablespoons water. Cook 2 to 3 minutes.

Serve with a hearty whole grain bread.

37. Rice with mixed vegies

Cook ¾ cup brown rice with 2 tablespoons sesame seeds.

Prepare for cooking a combination of the following vegies totaling 2 cups: broccoli, zucchini, celery, green peppers, onion and Chinese cabbage.

Saute vegies in 1 tablespoon oil mixed with 1 tablespoon soy sauce during the last 10 minutes the rice is cooking.

Serve the vegies over the rice.

38. Eggplant Parmesan

Cook brown rice according to basic recipe.

Place 6 slices of peeled eggplant on a thinly oiled pan and bake 10 minutes at 400°.

Meanwhile, mix and saute in a cast iron pan:

½ cup tomato sauce

1 teaspoon parsley flakes and 1 bay leaf

1/8 teaspoon each of oregano, rosemary and thyme

1 minced clove garlic and 1 small chopped onion

1 tablespoon chopped green onion

Pour the sauteed mixture over the eggplant and sprinkle with 3 tablespoons Parmesan cheese, 4 tablespoons sesame seeds and 4 ounces of Mozarella or Swiss cheese.

Bake 20 minutes at 375°. Serve over rice.

39. Key lime fish

Beat 1 egg with 2 tablespoons lime juice. Pour over 8 ounces of whiting or any frozen fish.

Place in a greased pan and sprinkle with 1 crumbled slice of whole wheat bread.

Bake for 25 minutes at 400°.

Serve with quick biscuits and steamed vegies.

176

40. Corn & bean casserole

Saute in 1 tablespoon oil:

1 chopped onion

1 chopped carrot

1 stalk chopped celery

Mix 1 cup cornmeal with 2 tablespoons sesame seeds. Mix with sauteed vegies and add 1 tablespoon soy sauce, ¼ cup grated cheese and 1 cup cooked beans—kidney, pinto, chick peas, etc.

Bake 20 minutes at 375°.

Serve with a salad of your choice.

41. Rutabaga & beef

Cook all day on low heat or in a slow cooker (or 30 minutes in a pressure cooker):

1 small rutabaga, peeled, cut in medium cubes

4 to 8 ounces beef roast

2 cups water

Ten minutes before meal time, steam ½ cup each of cauliflower and frozen or fresh lima beans.

Just prior to serving, remove rutabaga, add ½ cup warm milk or cream and blenderize.

Serve rutabaga on the side.

42. Fish & things

Place in pressure cooker with 2 cups water:
2 chopped potatoes
½ cup corn
1 chopped carrot and 1 chopped onion
1 stalk chopped parsley
1 or 2 chopped beets
1 package gelatin
1 cup oatmeal
½ teaspoon each oregano and basil
Cook at 15 pounds pressure for 15 minutes.
Saute 4 to 6 ounces of fish in 1 ounce oil and ½ cup water. Add 1 tablespoon soy sauce.
Serve with vegies and Parmesan cheese.

43. Peanut noodles

Saute 1 chopped onion in 1 tablespoon oil and ¼ teaspoon cayenne. Whisk in:
1½ tablespoons arrowroot flour
1 cup milk or yogurt
½ teaspoon dry mustard
1/8 teaspoon pepper
Add 1 cup chopped peanuts. Serve over 2 cups cooked whole wheat noodles with a green salad.

44. Chili con carne

Brown 8 ounces ground meat in ½ tablespoon oil in a pressure cooker. Add:
½ cup tomato juice
½ cup chopped onion
1 teaspoon chili powder
1 cup canned kidney beans
Cook 15 minutes at 15 pounds pressure.
Serve with flat bread and a salad.

45. Spinach and tofu pie

Mix well in a bowl: 1 cup whole wheat flour, ¼ teaspoon salt, and 1 ounce each butter and oil. Add 2 ounces cold water and work into a dough ball. Roll to a thin crust and place in a greased pan. Prick with fork in several places and bake 5 to 10 minutes at 400°.

Meanwhile, saute 1 chopped onion in 1 tablespoon oil in a cast iron pan. Add 1½ cups frozen or chopped fresh spinach.

Mix 1½ cups crumbled tofu with one-half clove minced garlic and 1 teaspoon lemon juice. Add to onions and spinach, mix well and pour into pie crust. Bake 20 minutes at 400°.

46. Chicken soup

Place in a pressure cooker with 4 cups water:
1 pound chicken, cut in serving pieces
½ cup rice
1 chopped carrot
1 chopped onion
1 stalk chopped celery
1/8 teaspoon pepper
Cook at 15 pounds pressure for 15 minutes.
Serve with salad and flat bread.

47. Vegetarian peppers

Saute in 1 tablespoon oil:
1 small chopped onion
1 stalk chopped celery
½ cup tomato sauce
½ teaspoon basil
1 teaspoon chopped parsley
Mix with ¼ cup grated cheese and ½ cup cooked and mashed dried beans—pinto, kidney, chick peas, etc.

Stuff mixture into 2 cored green peppers.

Place peppers in cast iron pan with 1½ cups water. Bake at 400° for 20 minutes.

48. Beerbit

Saute 1 heaping tablespoon arrowroot flour and ½ teaspoon dry mustard in 1 tablespoon oil, whisking. Add ½ cup beer at room temperature and whisk as it cooks.

Stir in 1 cup grated cheese, ½ teaspoon horseradish and ¼ teaspoon pepper.

Serve over toasted whole wheat English muffins or bagels with side dishes of steamed zucchini, asparagus, broccoli or edible podded peas.

Sharp cheddar is best.

49. Friday night fish

Cook ¾ cup brown rice.

Saute 1 tablespoon arrowroot flour in 1 tablespoon oil, whisking. Add:

1 chopped onion and 1 chopped carrot

1 stalk chopped celery

1 cup milk

¼ teaspoon salt and 1/8 teaspoon dry mustard

½ cup each of mushrooms, cauliflower and creamed corn

4 to 6 ounces of fish

Serve with the rice.

50. Spaghetti & meatballs #2

Saute in 1 tablespoon oil:
1 chopped onion and 1 chopped green pepper
1 teaspoon each oregano, salt and chili powder or hot peppers
½ teaspoon each basil, cumin and salt
1 bay leaf and one-half clove garlic
Mix 2 ounces ground pork with 2 ounces ground beef. Add one-half chopped onion and ¼ teaspoon oregano. Make into small meatballs and add to onion and green pepper mixture. Add 1 tablespoon soy sauce and 1 cup tomato sauce.

Cook slowly while you prepare the spaghetti.

Cook whole wheat or soy wheat spaghetti in boiling water. Serve with meatball sauce and a green or fruit salad.

51. Legumes & cheese

Cook ¾ cup brown rice.

Saute in 1 tablespoon oil: 1 chopped onion, 1 clove chopped garlic, 2 ounces chile peppers, ½ cup cooked chick peas and 4 ounces cheese—cheddar, Monterey Jack, Swiss or farmers.

Serve over the rice.

182

52. Tuna loaf

Heat ¾ cup milk to scalding. Crumble 2 slices whole wheat bread and mix with milk. Add:

1 teaspoon each oil and butter
6½ ounces water packed tuna
1 chopped onion and 1 stalk chopped celery
½ teaspoon chopped parsley

Mix in 2 beaten egg yolks. Fold in 2 egg whites that have been beaten until fluffy.

Pour into a greased pan and bake 25 minutes at 375°.

Serve with steamed spinach, cauliflower, broccoli or zucchini.

53. Barley casserole

Boil together, then simmer for 25 to 30 minutes:

1 tablespoon soy sauce
1 teaspoon lemon juice
1 chopped onion
4 ounces mushrooms
⅔ cup barley
2 ounces ground beef
1 cup water

Serve with steamed vegies or a green salad.

54. Rabbit Stroganoff

Cook ½ to ¾ cup whole grains.

Cube 8 ounces of rabbit meat and roll in 2 table-spoons fine cornmeal.

Saute 1 chopped onion and 1 chopped clove of garlic in 1 tablespoon each of oil and water. Add rabbit cubes and cook until brown. Stir in:

4 ounces of mushrooms

1 tablespoon soy sauce

1 tablespoon parsley

1 teaspoon basil

Just prior to serving, stir in 2 tablespoons cream cheese and 4 ounces yogurt. Serve over whole grains with a green salad or steamed vegies.

55. Spinach & rice

Cook ¾ cup brown rice.

Saute 1 chopped onion and 1 package of frozen spinach in 1 tablespoon oil. Stir in:

1 beaten egg

½ cup grated cheese

1/8 teaspoon pepper

1 tablespoon ground sesame seeds

Serve over the rice.

56. Garbanzoes & rutabaga

Mix in a pressure cooker:
½ cup cooked garbanzoes or chick peas
1 cup chopped rutabaga
one-half small chopped cabbage
½ cup fresh spinach
one-half clove of minced garlic
Cook 15 minutes at 15 pounds pressure. Meanwhile, saute in 1 tablespoon oil:
1 chopped onion
2 tablespoons chopped basil
¼ cup grated cheese
Add 1 cup of milk and simmer. Add the garbanzo and rutabaga mixture to the "soup" stock.
Serve with popcorn floating in the soup.

57. Fish chowder

Saute 1 chopped onion and 2 finely chopped potatoes in:
1 tablespoon oil and 2 tablespoons water
Stir in 4 to 8 ounces of fish and ¼ teaspoon salt.
Add 2 cups warm milk and simmer 20 minutes.
Serve with a green salad and whole wheat crackers.

58. Winter squash casserole

Peel and slice thinly (a food processor does it best) a small acorn squash—or pumpkin, butternut or turban squash. Saute squash with 1 chopped onion in 1 tablespoon oil and 2 tablespoons water, until lightly browned.

Beat 2 eggs with:

1 tablespoon arrowroot or whole wheat flour

a dash of nutmeg

¼ cup sour cream or yogurt (if using yogurt, add 1 teaspoon honey)

Mix with squash and divide into 2 greased pudding dishes. Bake at 375° for 15 to 20 minutes.

Serve with cranberry sauce.

Cranberry sauce

Place 1 cup washed cranberries in a pot with 2 tablespoons honey and 1 teaspoon orange juice concentrate (optional). Cook on high until berries start to pop, then turn to simmer and cover.

If you like it very thick, add 1 teaspoon guar gum and stir well.

Make extra—it keeps for several weeks in the refrigerator. It's a wonderful relish for most meats. Serve on the side.

59. Lasagna

Cook ½ pound spinach lasagna in 1 quart boiling water. Meanwhile, blenderize 6 ounces of tomato sauce with ¼ cup water and:

1 small onion or several scallions
1 tablespoon parsley and 1 teaspoon basil
½ teaspoon oregano and ¼ teaspoon marjoram
1 clove garlic

Spread in layers in a greased loaf pan: half of the lasagna, half of the tomato sauce, 2 ounces Ricotta cheese, 1 ounce ground beef, and 2 tablespoons wheat germ. Repeat, using rest of ingredients.

Top with 1 ounce grated Mozarella and 1 ounce Parmesan cheese. Bake at 375° for 25 minutes.

Serve with a green salad.

60. Scalloped fish

Place in greased cast iron pan: 4 to 8 ounces fish (cut in small cubes), 1 tablespoon chopped green pepper, 6 ounces green peas, 1 tablespoon lemon juice, 2 finely chopped potatoes and 1 tablespoon soy sauce. Top with ¼ cup grated cheese.

Bake at 400° for 30 minutes.

Serve with a green or fruit salad.

61. Rice with cheese

Cook ¾ cup of brown rice. When rice reaches bubble stage, add 1 cup of zucchini, broccoli, eggplant, cabbage, Chinese cabbage, *or* edible podded peas. Cover and simmer.

Five minutes before the rice is done, saute 1 chopped onion, 1 beaten egg, the juice of one-half lemon, ¼ teaspoon pepper and ¼ cup grated cheese in 1 tablespoon of oil.

Serve vegies and rice with the cheese sauce.

62. Legume loaf

Cook 1 cup mixed grains—wheat, oats, rye, rice, millet, etc.

Mix 1 cup mashed cooked beans—chick peas or soy beans are best—with 1 minced clove garlic, 1 chopped onion and 1 beaten egg.

Mix beans with grains. Add 4 ounces chopped mushrooms. Bake in greased loaf pan at 375° for 15 to 20 minutes. Meanwhile:

Saute 1 small chopped onion in 1 tablespoon oil. Whisk in 1 tablespoon arrowroot flour, 1 cup milk and 2 tablespoons chopped parsley.

Serve sauce over loaf with a fruit salad.

63. Curried chicken

Cook ½ to ¾ cup brown rice.
Saute in 1 tablespoon each of oil and water:
1 chopped onion and 2 minced cloves of garlic
1/8 teaspoon cloves and ½ tablespoon minced ginger root (or 1 teaspoon dry ginger)
½ teaspoon each of cumin, chili powder, curry powder, cinnamon and cardamon
Stir in 4 to 6 ounces of cubed chicken, ½ cup yogurt, 1 cup water, 1 cup canned or frozen green peas and 1 cup frozen cauliflower.
Simmer until rice is done. Serve over the rice with raisins, slivered almonds, sliced banana, mango chutney and unsweetened coconut.

64. Tofu sukiyaki

Cook ¾ cup brown rice. Meanwhile, saute 1 chopped onion in 1 tablespoon each oil and water.
Add 1 ounce cooking sherry, 2 tablespoons soy sauce, 4 ounces chopped Chinese cabbage, 2 ounces of mushrooms and 1 teaspoon honey.
Cook 5 minutes, then add 4 to 6 ounces of tofu cut into cubes. Simmer until rice is done.
Serve sukiyaki over rice.

65. Lentil pate

Cook ¾ cup lentils and 1½ cups water all day in a slow cooker.

In the evening, saute in 1 tablespoon each of oil and water:

1 chopped onion

1 chopped clove garlic

2 tablespoons chopped or dry parsley

Stir in 2 slices crumbled dry bread. Add 1 heaping teaspoon dill weed and 1/8 teaspoon pepper.

Blenderize lentils and onion mixture with 1 egg and ½ teaspoon soy sauce. Pour into a greased pan and bake at 375° for 20 minutes.

Serve with steamed cauliflower, kohlrabi, brussels sprouts, mushrooms or Jerusalem artichokes.

If you make a double recipe, you can use the leftovers for pate sandwiches. Stuff in pocket bread with alfalfa sprouts.

66. Salmon loaf

Saute 1 chopped onion, 1 stalk chopped celery and 1 clove garlic in 1 tablespoon each of oil and water. Add this mixture to:

6 ounces pink, red or coho canned salmon
2 slices crumbled bread
1 tablespoon each chopped parsley and basil
½ teaspoon dill weed

Mix well and add 2 beaten eggs, 2 to 4 ounces plain yogurt and 1 tablespoon lemon juice.

Mix thoroughly and pour into a greased loaf pan. Bake at 375° for 25 minutes. Serve with steamed snow peas and whole grain buns.

67. Spiced chicken livers

Cook ½ to ¾ cup brown rice.

Saute 2 chopped shallots or 1 small onion in 1 tablespoon each of oil and water. After 5 minutes, add 4 to 8 ounces of chicken livers.

Saute 3 minutes, then add ½ teaspoon allspice, ½ teapoon ground or 1 teaspoon fresh chopped ginger, 1 teaspoon soy sauce and 1 tablespoon raisins.

Serve over rice with fresh fruit or green salad.

68. Tofu with kale

Cook ½ to ¾ cup brown rice or millet.
Saute in 1 tablespoon each of oil and water:
1 chopped onion
½ clove chopped garlic
6 to 8 ounces tofu, cubed
Simmer while rice cooks. When rice begins to bubble, add 4 to 6 ounces kale on top and cover.
Serve tofu over rice, with kale on top of tofu. Sprinkle with 1 tablespoon soy sauce, 2 tablespoons ground sesame seeds and 1 tablespoon grated Parmesan cheese.
Or try chard, beet greens or spinach in place of kale.

69. Shrimp & crab stew

Cook rice or pressure cook small potatoes.
Saute in 1 tablespoon each of oil and water: 1 small chopped onion, 1 small chopped carrot, 1 chopped stalk celery, one-half chopped apple and 2 tablespoons parsley. Add:
3 ounces bay shrimp
3 ounces canned crabmeat
¼ teaspoon thyme and a dash of nutmeg
Serve over rice or potatoes with fresh fruit salad.

70. Rabbit Versailles

Cook ½ to ¾ cup rice or grains.

Saute in 1 tablespoon each of oil and water:

1 chopped onion

6 to 8 ounces cubed rabbit

When rabbit is nearly done, ignite 1 tablespoon brandy or bourbon in a separate, preheated, greased cast iron skillet. Shake pan until flames cease. Stir in 3 to 4 ounces heavy cream and continue stirring until slightly thickened.

Mix sauce and rabbit and serve over rice with steamed vegies or green salad.

71. Mixed bean stew

Mixes in 5 minutes—but can cook as long as 6 to 8 hours!

Mix together ⅓ cup each of chick peas, lima beans and navy beans. Add 2 cups water plus:

4 to 8 ounces lean beef chunks (stew, roast, steak)

1 chopped onion and 1 clove garlic

4 ounces tomato sauce and 1 bay leaf

Simmer on stove or in a slow cooker all day, or cook in 30 minutes at 15 pounds pressure in a pressure cooker.

Serve with whole wheat bread and green salad.

72. Macaroni & shrimp

Cook 4 to 6 ounces whole wheat or soya wheat macaroni (or noodles) in 3 cups boiling water.

Saute in 1 tablespoon each of oil and water:

1 chopped clove garlic

1 chopped onion or 4 chopped scallions

1 stalk chopped celery

1 tablespoon chopped pimento

1 teaspoon dill weed

4 to 6 ounces bay shrimp

Beat 1 egg with ½ cup milk. Mix with shrimp mixture and macaroni. Pour into greased casserole and bake at 400° for 20 minutes.

Serve with a green salad.

73. Spinach pie

Beat 3 eggs with ½ cup milk, ½ cup whole wheat flour and ½ teaspoon baking powder.

Stir in ½ cup crumbled cheese and 4 to 6 ounces chopped spinach.

Pour into a greased 6" or 8" Pyrex pie plate.

Cook at 400° for 20 minutes or until browned.

Serve alone or with a fruit or green salad.

Chopped broccoli is a good alternative to spinach.

74. Cornbread meat pie

Saute in 1 tablespoon each of oil and water:
4 ounces ground pork or beef
1 chopped onion
2 tablespoons chopped green pepper
Meanwhile, blenderize ½ cup cornmeal with:
½ cup milk and ½ cup sour cream or yogurt
1 tablespoon honey and 1 egg
1 tablespoon oil and ½ teaspoon baking powder
¼ cup whole wheat flour
Mix meat and cornmeal mixtures and pour into greased custard cups. Bake 20 minutes at 400°.
Serve with steamed vegies or green salad.

75. Rice with herb sauce

Cook ½ to ¾ cup brown rice.
Saute 1 chopped onion in 1 tablespoon each oil and water. Add 1 tablespoon lemon juice plus:
1/8 teaspoon pepper and 1 beaten egg
2 tablespoons ground sesame seeds
1 tablespoon dry or fresh chopped basil
2 tablespoons Parmesan cheese
Stir briefly and then serve over rice with fresh fruit or green salad.

76. Lima bean curry

Cook ¾ cup dried lima beans and 2 cups water all day on low heat in a slow cooker.

In the evening, cook ¾ cup millet or rice.

Saute 1 chopped onion in 1 tablespoon each of oil and water. Add:

1/8 teaspoon each of turmeric and curry powder
¼ teaspoon cloves and 1 chopped tart apple

Beat 1 tablespoon arrowroot flour and 1 tablespoon soy sauce into 1 cup of milk. Add to onion mixture and stir over low heat until thickened.

Blend in beans and serve over millet or rice.

Raisins, dates, figs and slices of orange, tangerine, grapefruit and banana complement this curry nicely.

77. French fish

Cook ¾ cup brown rice, millet or any grain.
Place 8 ounces of fish into a cast iron pan with:
2 ounces dry white wine or vermouth
1 chopped onion and 1 tablespoon oil
1 tablespoon parsley and ½ teaspoon thyme
1 tablespoon chopped chives or scallions
Bake at 375° for 20 minutes. Serve over the rice with steamed vegie vegies.

78. Kidney with apple

Combine in a slow cooker or pressure cooker:
4 to 6 ounces chopped kidney
1 chopped onion or 1 bunch scallions
1 tablespoon oil
1 chopped apple
4 to 6 small potatoes
1 cup milk and 1 cup water
a splash of red wine
Cook all day in slow cooker or 25 minutes in the pressure cooker. When done, stir in 1 tablespoon arrowroot flour whisked with 2 ounces water.

Add vegies. Steam vegies while liquid thickens. Or steam vegies on the side.

Chopped heart can be substituted for the kidney. All organ meats are delicacies. For variety, try chicken, lamb and veal organs, as well as beef and pork.

79. Humus pocket taco

Blenderize 4 tablespoons sesame seeds, 1 clove garlic, 1 tablespoon oil, 1 tablespoon lemon juice and ¼ teaspoon each of salt, coriander and cumin.

Add 1 cup cooked chick peas and ½ cup yogurt. Stuff humus and greens into pocket bread.

197

80. Sukiyaki

Soak 1 package (3¾ ounces) of cellophane noodles in hot water.

Saute in 1 tablespoon each of oil and water:
1 bunch chopped scallions or 2 onions
4 to 6 ounces boned, cubed chicken
1 tablespoon sesame seeds

When browned, add 4 ounces chopped broccoli, 1 tablespoon soy sauce, one half of a chopped red pepper, 1 tablespoon chopped fresh ginger and 4 to 6 ounces chopped or frozen spinach. Cook 10 minutes and top with noodles, cut in 2-inch lengths.

For a heavier meal, serve sukiyaki over brown rice, with a key lime pie for dessert.

81. Spanish fish

Saute ½ cup rice in 2 tablespoons oil with 1 chopped onion, 1 minced clove garlic, one half chopped green or red pepper, 4 ounces canned mushrooms and juice, 4 ounces tomato sauce, ½ cup water, 4 to 6 ounces tuna or other fish and a dash of cayenne or hot sauce.

Cook briskly until liquid is mostly evaporated. Cover and simmer until rice is fluffy.

82. Meatless spaghetti

Cook whole wheat or soybean spaghetti in boiling water. Meanwhile, saute 1 chopped onion and 1 chopped clove garlic in 1 tablespoon each of oil and water. Add and simmer 5 to 10 minutes:
¼ cup soy grits and 6 ounces tomato sauce
2 tablespoons ground sesame or sunflower seeds
2 tablespoons peanut butter
½ teaspoon oregano and 1 teaspoon soy sauce
1 tablespoon dried parsley
1 ounce red wine and 2 to 4 ounces mushrooms
Serve sauce over drained spaghetti with 1 to 2 tablespoons Parmesan cheese and a green salad.

83. Beef cake

Saute in 1 tablespoon each oil and water:
1 chopped onion and 1 tablespoon parsley
4 to 6 ounces ground beef (or any lean meat)
Process 1 raw sweet potato and 1 carrot until finely chopped. Beat in 1 egg, then add sweet potato mixture to beef, mixing well.

Pour into greased custard cups and bake at 375° for 20 minutes. Serve with quick biscuits and a green salad or steamed vegies.

84. Stew

Cook ½ cup brown rice or millet.

Saute 1 chopped onion, 1 can chopped green chili peppers and ¼ teaspoon chili powder in 1 tablespoon each of oil and water.

Add 2 to 4 ounces stewed tomatoes, 2 to 4 ounces corn, 2 to 4 ounces green beans and ½ cup cooked or canned soybeans. If you wish, add 1 to 3 ounces of any leftover meat for flavor.

Serve over rice or millet.

If necessary, cook soybeans all day in a slow cooker.

85. Beans & spinach

Cook ¾ cup navy or pinto beans and 2 cups water all day in a slow cooker.

In the evening, cook ½ to ¾ cup brown rice.

Saute 1 clove garlic and 1 small onion in 1 tablespoon each of oil and water. Add 4 to 6 ounces chopped spinach and stir fry for 5 minutes.

Add beans with 1 cup of their liquid, 1 chopped hot pepper, a pinch of cayenne and 1/8 teaspoon pepper. Simmer 15 minutes, then add 1 tablespoon soy sauce and serve over rice.

Or use canned beans and fix entirely in the evening.

86. Shrimp Thermidor

Cook ½ to ¾ cup brown rice or grains.

Saute 1 chopped onion in 1 tablespoon each of oil and water in a cast iron pan.

Whisk 1 cup milk and 2 tablespoons arrowroot flour. Add 2 ounces dry white wine. Add mixture to onion and stir or whisk on low heat until thick.

Add 4 ounces chopped fish and 2 to 4 ounces bay shrimp. Stir in 2 ounces grated Mozzarella and 2 tablespoons grated Parmesan cheese.

Simmer or bake in oven at 400° until rice is cooked. Serve with steamed vegies over rice.

87. Baked beans

Simmer 1 cup kidney or navy beans in 2 cups of water during the day. Pour off water in evening.

Fry 3 slices of nitrate-free bacon in a pressure cooker. Pour off fat and add cooked beans with:

½ cup frozen orange juice concentrate

1 tablespoon each molasses and dry sherry

¼ cup tomato sauce and 1/8 teaspoon ginger

¼ teaspoon dry mustard and water to cover

Cook at 15 pounds pressure for 25 minutes.

Or use nitrate-free weiners or soy sausages for the bacon.

88. Slow cooker Spanish rice

Saute 1 stalk chopped celery, 1 clove chopped garlic, 1 chopped onion and 1 chopped green pepper in 1 tablespoon each of oil and water in a slow cooker. Add 2 cups water plus:

⅓ cup rice and 1 tablespoon dry soy beans
2 tablespoons peanuts or cashews
1 cup canned tomatoes and ¼ teaspoon oregano
1 tablespoon arrowroot flour
2 to 4 ounces mushrooms

Cook slowly all day. In the evening, crumble 2 ounces sharp cheddar or 2 tablespoons Parmesan over the rice, 5 minutes before serving.

Serve with green or fruit salad.

89. Baked turbot

Place 8 ounces turbot in a greased pan. Pour over it a mixture of 2 heaping tablespoons frozen orange juice concentrate and ¼ teaspoon each of dill weed, garlic powder, rosemary and thyme.

Bake at 425° for 25 minutes.

Meanwhile, cook 4 small to medium potatoes, quartered, at 15 pounds in a pressure cooker.

Serve turbot and potatoes with steamed vegies.

90. Dilled fish

Place 6 to 8 ounces of fish in a greased cast iron pan. Pour over the fish a sauce made of:
½ cup yogurt and 1 tablespoon lemon juice
1 tablespoon parsley and 1 chopped onion
1 heaping teaspoon dill weed
1 tablespoon oil and 1/8 teaspoon pepper
Bake at 425° for 20 minutes.
Cook brown rice in usual way, steaming zucchini on top once rice reaches bubble stage.
Serve fish and rice with greens.

91. Bean curd chop suey

Cook ½ to ¾ cup mixed grains or rice.
Saute in 1 tablespoon each of oil and water:
1 chopped onion and 1 stalk chopped celery
one fourth of a green pepper, chopped
½ teaspoon fresh chopped or ¼ teaspoon dried ginger and 1 tablespoon soy sauce
4 ounces cubed tofu and ¼ cup water
Add small amounts of snow peas, cauliflower, zucchini, Chinese cabbage and mushrooms—or any other vegie vegie that can be steamed.
Serve over the rice with Chinese noodles.

92. Meat pie

Blenderize 1 cup milk with 2 eggs. Add:
1 small onion and 1 carrot
1 tablespoon arrowroot flour
1 stalk celery and 2 ounces of cheese
½ cup whole wheat flour
Blend well and pour over 4 ounces chopped or cubed meat of any kind—lean pork, chicken, beef, or turkey.

Bake in greased pan at 400° for 30 minutes.
Serve with a green salad or fruit.

93. Cold salmon loaf

Blenderize 1 cup warm milk with 1 package plain gelatin (1 tablespoon). Add:
½ cup mayonnaise and ¼ teaspoon pepper
1 small onion and 1 stalk celery
1 tablespoon of soy, Worcestershire or Heinz 57 sauce
6½ ounces canned salmon
Pour into 2 greased pottery cups without handles, or custard cups. Freeze for 20 to 30 minutes.

Serve on greens with hot muffins or biscuits.
Tuna or sardines can be used instead of salmon.

DESSERTS

In general, I recommend few of the standard types of desserts. However, almost everyone likes something sweet at the end of a meal. Here are some ideas for speedy desserts that can be fixed in less than five minutes:

Mix together almonds, figs, dates and raisins. This is a super mix!

Serve any fresh fruit with real whipped cream on top. You can afford the whipped cream once or twice a week because your diet is so good!

The three recipes for ice cream I give can also be fixed in less than five minutes.

Many of the more elaborate desserts I fix require a pie crust. There are several ways of making a quickie crust. Here are my favorites:

Granola pie crust

Mix 2 cups granola with 4 ounces cream cheese or 2 tablespoons each of oil and soft butter. Press into a greased pie plate (I prefer Pyrex).

Nutty pie crust

Mix 1 cup ground pecans or almonds, 1 cup sesame seeds and 2 to 3 ounces of cream cheese. Press into a greased pie plate.

Wheat germ crust

Mix 1 cup wheat germ with 1 tablespoon honey and 4 ounces soft butter or 2 ounces each butter and cream cheese. Press into an 8-inch pie plate.

Any of these three pie crusts may be baked 5 minutes at 375° before filling.

Whole wheat crust #1

Place ⅓ cup whole wheat pastry flour or blenderized whole wheat flour in a mixing bowl. Beat in ¼ cup refrigerated butter. Stir in:

1 tablespoon honey

½ teaspoon vanilla extract

1½ cups finely chopped nuts—pecans, walnuts or almonds

Stir to make a soft dough and press thinly and evenly into a greased 9-inch pie plate. Refrigerate while making filling or bake 5 minutes at 425° for a precooked crust.

Whole wheat crust #2

Mix 1½ cups whole wheat flour (blenderize until fine) with ¼ teaspoon salt. Pour into mixing bowl.

In a separate bowl, mix ¼ cup safflower oil with:

1 beaten egg

½ tablespoon cider vinegar

2 tablespoons cold water

Mix the liquid into the flour with a whisk. When well mixed, knead into a ball, roll thinly on a flour board and place into a greased, 9-inch pie plate. Prick bottom with a fork in several places. Bake at least 2 or 3 minutes (for an uncooked crust) or 10 minutes at 425° for a cooked crust.

To top a pie, such as an apple pie, with crust, just double the recipe. Most pies need only the bottom crust.

And now for the recipes of some truly irresistible desserts.

1. Pumpkin cheesecake

Beat 8 ounces of room-temperature cream cheese. Add 3 eggs, 1 at a time, then:

1½ cups cooked pumpkin

½ cup maple syrup or honey

¼ teaspoon almond extract

2 teaspoons vanilla extract

Mix thoroughly, then pour into a baked pie crust and bake at 400° for 10 minutes. Lower temperature to 325° and bake for 30 minutes more, until well browned. If not too brown, turn off oven and let cheesecake cool in the oven.

Top with sour cream, whipped cream or yogurt.

Try winter squash or sweet potato instead of pumpkin.

2. Pecan pie

Cream ¼ cup butter in a mixing bowl. Add:

3 eggs, 1 at a time, and ½ cup warm honey

2 tablespoons milk and 1 teaspoon vanilla

1 tablespoon arrowroot or whole wheat flour

Pour 1 cup pecan halves or pieces into a 9-inch uncooked pie crust. Pour custard mixture over pecans and bake 30 to 40 minutes at 350°. Test center with knife, which should come out clean.

3. Key lime pie

Whisk together 1½ cups honey and 6 tablespoons arrowroot flour in top of a double boiler.

Blend in ½ cup cold water and ½ cup key lime juice (or lemon or grapefruit juice). Gradually add:

3 well beaten eggs

2 tablespoons butter

1½ cups boiling water

Bring to a full boil while stirring or whisking gently, until it thickens. Stir in 1 teaspoon grated lime peel and pour into a baked pie crust.

Bake at 325° for 30 to 45 minutes.

May be removed 10 minutes before its done, covered with a meringue of beaten egg whites, and returned to oven to brown meringue.

Chill before serving.

4. Quickie cheese cake

Cream 24 ounces cream cheese in a bowl with:

4 tablespoons lemon juice and 1 teaspoon vanilla

2 to 4 tablespoons honey

1 tablespoon guar gum

Pour into a cooked flour crust or pressed crust.

Chill. Serve as is or with fruit toppings.

5. Cheesecake

Cream 24 ounces of cream cheese in a mixing bowl. Slowly add:
¾ cup honey
¼ teaspoon salt
2 tablespoons arrowroot flour
1 teaspoon vanilla extract
1 tablespoon lemon juice
1 teaspoon grated lemon rind
4 eggs, 1 at a time
Pour into uncooked 9″ pie crust and bake 45 minutes at 350°. Cool in oven with door open.
Chill before serving.

6. Coffee ice cream

Place in the blender:
1 cup whipping cream
1 tablespoon honey
2 teaspoons decaffeinated coffee
2 cups cracked ice
a few almonds
For a mocha taste, add chocolate or carob.
Blenderize and serve.
Rombouts is an especially good decaffeinated coffee.

7. Apple pie

Slice 4 cups of apples onto an uncooked pie crust. Mix together:
⅓ cup honey
1 tablespoon oil or melted butter
½ teaspoon each cinnamon and nutmeg
2 tablespoons arrowroot or whole wheat flour
Pour evenly over the apples.
Top with a rolled pie crust (prick well) or oatmeal, chopped nuts, cheddar cheese or granola.
Bake at 350° for 45 minutes until well browned.
Serve with whipped cream or cheese slices.

8. Tofu cheesecake

Blenderize 1 tablespoon sesame seeds. Add:
1 tablespoon oil
20 ounces of tofu
2 tablespoons honey and ¼ cup raisins
1 teaspoon vanilla and 2 eggs
1 tablespoon lemon juice
Pour into uncooked or partly cooked pie crust. Bake at 350° for 25 minutes. Cool well before serving, preferably overnight in refrigerator.
Excellent with fruit topping.

9. Fruit cake

Cream 1 cup butter with 1 cup honey. Add 7 eggs, 1 at a time.

Mix separately: ½ cup Welch's grape juice, ½ cup molasses and 2 teaspoons vanilla.

Mix separately: 2½ cups raisins, 2 cups walnuts or other nuts, 7 cups dried fruit—citron, chopped dates or figs, candied fruits—and 1 cup flour.

Mix separately: 5 cups *blenderized* whole wheat flour, 1 tablespoon each of cinnamon and allspice, 1 teaspoon each of ground cloves, ground nutmeg and salt, 1½ teaspoons baking powder and 1½ cups dry oatmeal.

Blend all mixtures together and pour into a greased bundt pan or tubular cake pan covered with greased brown paper. Bake 2½ to 3 hours at 250°, *until knife comes out clean.*

Or shorten baking time by baking in a regular bread pan.

10. Ice cream liqueur

Place in blender 1 cup whipping cream, 1 tablespoon honey, and 2 to 4 ounces of any liqueur—creme de menthe, creme de cacao, Kahlúa, etc.

Add 2 cups chopped ice, blenderize and serve.

11. Homemade "Oreos"

Cream 1 cup butter with 1 cup honey and 1 egg.
Add slowly ¾ cup cocoa plus:
2½ cups blenderized whole wheat flour
¼ teaspoon baking powder and ½ teaspoon salt
1 teaspoon vanilla
When well mixed, roll dough fairly thin and cut into rounds—preferably with a donut cutter.
Bake on greased cookie sheet at 400° until crisp (about 15 minutes). Remove with spatula to cool.
While cooling, mix 4 ounces cream cheese, 2 tablespoons honey and 1 teaspoon vanilla.
Spread onto half of the cooled cookies and complete sandwiches with other half.

12. Laurel's cheese cake

Stir 1 package plain gelatin (1 tablespoon) into 1 cup boiling water. Add ½ cup honey. Beat in:
16 ounces cream cheese and 1 egg
1 tablespoon lemon or lime juice
Pour into precooked or pressed pie crust.
Chill in refrigerator 2 hours or freezer 1 hour.
Serve as is or with fruit topping.
Using the lime juice is a quick way to make a key lime pie.

13. Fruit ice cream

Heat 1 cup apple juice with 1 package plain gelatin (1 tablespoon). Pour into blender with 1 cup whipping cream and 1 egg. Start blender and drop in frozen fruit—strawberries, blueberries, peaches or bananas—until mixture is thick.

For a sherbet, omit the cream and/or egg—or substitute 1 cup yogurt and 1 tablespoon honey.

You can also substitute 3 to 4 tablespoons frozen orange juice concentrate and cracked ice for the frozen fruit.

14. Chocolate pound cake

Cream well 1 pound butter and ¼ pound cream cheese. Add slowly 2 cups warm honey, 9 eggs, 1 at a time, 2 tablespoons rum and 1 teaspoon vanilla. Mix separately:

2 cups each (sifted) rye and unbleached flour
½ cup rice bran and 1½ cups sifted baking cocoa
1 heaping teaspoon baking powder

Add slowly to butter mixture, beating constantly.

Grease a tube or loaf pan with butter and dust with flour. Pour batter into pan and bake 1 hour in a preheated 325° regular oven or 45 to 55 minutes at 300° in a convection oven. Test with knife.

APPENDIX

Recommended additional reading:

Bland, Jeffrey, *Nutraerobics*, Harper & Row, San Francisco, 1983.

Hall, Ross Hume, *Food for Nought*, Harper & Row, Hagerstown, Maryland, 1974.

Shealy, C. Norman, *90 Days to Self-Health*, Dial Press, New York, 1977.

All of these books, plus many more health products, are available from: Self-Health Systems of Brindabella Farms®, Route 1, Box 127, Fair Grove, Missouri 65648.

Other books consulted:

Brewster, Letitia, and Jacobson, Michael F., *The Changing American Diet*, Center for Science in the Public Interest, Washington, D.C., 1978.

U.S. Department of Agriculture, *Nutritive Value of Foods*, 1964.

Ronco, William, *Food Co-ops*, Beacon Press, Boston, 1974.

Food co-ops

For information and the latest directory of food co-ops, write to: *Food Co-op Nooz and Directory*, Loop College, Food Co-op Project, 64 Lake Street, Chicago, Illinois 60601.

If you do not have access to a co-op, you can order whole-grain cereals, pastas, flours and beans from: Little Bear Trading Co., Route 1, Box 266-A, Cochrane, WI 54622.